Statistics for Data Science

Leverage the power of statistics for Data Analysis, Classification, Regression, Machine Learning, and Neural Networks

James D. Miller

BIRMINGHAM - MUMBAI

Statistics for Data Science

First published: November 2017

Production reference: 1151117

Published by Packt Publishing Ltd.
Livery Place
35 Livery Street
Birmingham
B3 2PB, UK.
ISBN 978-1-78829-067-8

www.packtpub.com

Credits

Author
James D. Miller

Reviewers
James C. Mott

Commissioning Editor
Veena Pagare

Acquisition Editor
Tushar Gupta

Content Development Editor
Snehal Kolte

Technical Editor
Sayli Nikalje

Copy Editor
Tasneem Fatehi

Project Coordinator
Manthan Patel

Proofreader
Safis Editing

Indexer
Aishwarya Gangawane

Graphics
Tania Dutta

Production Coordinator
Deepika Naik

About the Author

James D. Miller, is an IBM certified expert, creative innovator and accomplished Director, Sr. Project Leader and Application/System Architect with +35 years of extensive applications and system design and development experience across multiple platforms and technologies. Experiences include introducing customers to new and sometimes disruptive technologies and platforms, integrating with IBM Watson Analytics, Cognos BI, TM1 and web architecture design, systems analysis, GUI design and testing, database modelling and systems analysis, design and development of OLAP, client/server, web and mainframe applications and systems utilizing: IBM Watson Analytics, IBM Cognos BI and TM1 (TM1 rules, TI, TM1Web and Planning Manager), Cognos Framework Manager, dynaSight-ArcPlan, ASP, DHTML, XML, IIS, MS Visual Basic and VBA, Visual Studio, PERL, SPLUNK, WebSuite, MS SQL Server, ORACLE, SYBASE Server, and so on.

Responsibilities have also included all aspects of Windows and SQL solution development and design including analysis; GUI (and website) design; data modelling; table, screen/form and script development; SQL (and remote stored procedures and triggers) development/testing; test preparation and management and training of programming staff. Other experience includes the development of **Extract**, **Transform**, and **Load** (**ETL**) infrastructure such as data transfer automation between mainframe (DB2, Lawson, Great Plains, and so on.) systems and client/server SQL server and web-based applications and integration of enterprise applications and data sources.

Mr Miller has acted as Internet Applications Development Mgr. responsible for the design, development, QA and delivery of multiple websites including online trading applications, warehouse process control and scheduling systems, administrative and control applications. Mr Miller also was responsible for the design, development and administration of a web-based financial reporting system for a 450-million-dollar organization, reporting directly to the CFO and his executive team.

He has also been responsible for managing and directing multiple resources in various management roles including project and team leader, lead developer and applications development director.

He has authored the following books published by Packt:

- *Mastering Predictive Analytics with R – Second Edition*
- *Big Data Visualization*
- *Learning IBM Watson Analytics*

- *Implementing Splunk – Second Edition*
- *Mastering Splunk*
- *IBM Cognos TM1 Developer's Certification Guide*

He has also authored a number of whitepapers on best practices such as *Establishing a Center of Excellence* and continues to post blogs on a number of relevant topics based on personal experiences and industry best practices.

He is a perpetual learner continuing to pursue experiences and certifications, currently holding the following current technical certifications:

- IBM Certified Developer Cognos TM1
- IBM Certified Analyst Cognos TM1
- IBM Certified Administrator Cognos TM1
- IBM Cognos TM1 Master 385 Certification
- IBM Certified Advanced Solution Expert Cognos TM1
- IBM OpenPages Developer Fundamentals C2020-001-ENU
- IBM Cognos 10 BI Administrator C2020-622
- IBM Cognos 10 BI Author C2090-620-ENU
- IBM Cognos BI Professional C2090-180-ENU
- IBM Cognos 10 BI Metadata Model Developer C2090-632
- IBM Certified Solution Expert - Cognos BI

Specialties: The evaluation and introduction of innovative and disruptive technologies, cloud migration, IBM Watson Analytics, big data, data visualizations, Cognos BI and TM1 application design and development, OLAP, Visual Basic, SQL Server, forecasting and planning; international application, and development, business intelligence, project development, and delivery and process improvement.

To Nanette L. Miller:
"Like a river flows surely to the sea, darling so it goes, some things are meant to be."

About the Reviewer

James Mott, Ph.D, is a senior education consultant with extensive experience in teaching statistical analysis, modeling, data mining and predictive analytics. He has over 30 years of experience using SPSS products in his own research including IBM SPSS Statistics, IBM SPSS Modeler, and IBM SPSS Amos. He has also been actively teaching these products to IBM/SPSS customers for over 30 years. In addition, he is an experienced historian with expertise in the research and teaching of 20th Century United States political history and quantitative methods. His specialties are data mining, quantitative methods, statistical analysis, teaching, and consulting.

www.PacktPub.com

For support files and downloads related to your book, please visit www.PacktPub.com.

Did you know that Packt offers eBook versions of every book published, with PDF and ePub files available? You can upgrade to the eBook version at www.PacktPub.com and as a print book customer, you are entitled to a discount on the eBook copy. Get in touch with us at service@packtpub.com for more details.

At www.PacktPub.com, you can also read a collection of free technical articles, sign up for a range of free newsletters and receive exclusive discounts and offers on Packt books and eBooks.

https://www.packtpub.com/mapt

Get the most in-demand software skills with Mapt. Mapt gives you full access to all Packt books and video courses, as well as industry-leading tools to help you plan your personal development and advance your career.

Why subscribe?

- Fully searchable across every book published by Packt
- Copy and paste, print, and bookmark content
- On demand and accessible via a web browser

Customer Feedback

Thanks for purchasing this Packt book. At Packt, quality is at the heart of our editorial process. To help us improve, please leave us an honest review on this book's Amazon page at https://www.amazon.com/dp/1788290674. If you'd like to join our team of regular reviewers, you can email us at customerreviews@packtpub.com. We award our regular reviewers with free eBooks and videos in exchange for their valuable feedback. Help us be relentless in improving our products!

Table of Contents

Preface

Statistics are an absolute must prerequisite for any task in the area of data science but may also be the most feared deterrent for developers entering into the field of data science. This book will take you on a statistical journey from knowing very little to becoming comfortable using various statistical methods for typical data science tasks.

What this book covers

Chapter 1: *Transitioning from Data Developer to Data Scientist*, sets the stage for the transition from data developer to data scientist. You will understand the difference between a developer mindset versus a data scientist mindset, the important difference between the two, and how to transition into thinking like a data scientist.

Chapter 2: *Declaring the Objectives*, introduces and explains (from a developer's perspective) the basic objectives behind statistics for data science and introduces you to the important terms and keys that are used in the field of data science.

Chapter 3: *A Developer's Approach to Data Cleaning*, discusses how a developer might understand and approach the topic of data cleaning using common statistical methods.

Chapter 4: *Data Mining and the Database Developer*, introduces the developer to mining data using R. You will understand what data mining is, why it is important, and feel comfortable using R for the most common statistical data mining methods: dimensional reduction, frequent patterns, and sequences.

Chapter 5: *Statistical Analysis for the Database Developer*, discusses the difference between data analysis or summarization and statistical data analysis and will follow the steps for successful statistical analysis of data, describe the nature of data, explore the relationships presented in data, create a summarization model from data, prove the validity of a model, and employ predictive analytics on a developed model.

Chapter 6: *Database Progression to Database Regression*, sets out to define statistical regression concepts and outline how a developer might use regression for simple forecasting and prediction within a typical data development project.

Chapter 7: *Regularization for Database Improvement*, introduces the developer to the idea of statistical regularization to improve data models. You will review what statistical regularization is, why it is important, and various statistical regularization methods.

Chapter 8: *Data Development and Assessment*, covers the idea of data model assessment and using statistics for assessment. You will understand what statistical assessment is, why it is important, and use R for statistical assessment.

Chapter 9: *Databases and Neural Networks*, defines the neural network model and draws from a developer's knowledge of data models to help understand the purpose and use of neural networks in data science.

Chapter 10: *Boosting and your Database*, introduces the idea of using statistical boosting to better understand data in a database.

Chapter 11: *Database Classification using Support Vector Machines*, uses developer terminologies to define an SVM, identify various applications for its use and walks through an example of using a simple SVM to classify data in a database

Chapter 12: *Database Structures and Machine Learning*, aims to provide an explanation of the types of machine learning and shows the developer how to use machine learning processes to understand database mappings and identify patterns within the data.

What you need for this book

This book is intended for those with a data development background who are interested in possibly entering the field of data science and are looking for concise information on the topic of statistics with the help of insightful programs and simple explanation. Just bring your data development experience and an open mind!

Who this book is for

This book is intended for those developers who are interested in entering the field of data science and are looking for concise information on the topic of statistics with the help of insightful programs and simple explanation.

Conventions

In this book, you will find a number of text styles that distinguish between different kinds of information. Here are some examples of these styles and an explanation of their meaning.

Code words in text, database table names, folder names, filenames, file extensions, pathnames, dummy URLs, user input, and Twitter handles are shown as follows: In statistics, a `boxplot` is a simple way to gain information regarding the shape, variability, and center (or median) of a statistical data set, so we'll use the `boxplot` with our data to see if we can identify both the median `Coin-in` and if there are any outliers.

A block of code is set as follows:

```
MyFile <-"C:/GammingData/SlotsResults.csv"
MyData <- read.csv(file=MyFile, header=TRUE, sep=",")
```

New terms and **important words** are shown in bold.

Warnings or important notes appear like this.

Tips and tricks appear like this.

Reader feedback

Feedback from our readers is always welcome. Let us know what you think about this book-what you liked or disliked. Reader feedback is important for us as it helps us develop titles that you will really get the most out of. To send us general feedback, simply email feedback@packtpub.com, and mention the book's title in the subject of your message. If there is a topic that you have expertise in and you are interested in either writing or contributing to a book, see our author guide at www.packtpub.com/authors.

Customer support

Now that you are the proud owner of a Packt book, we have a number of things to help you to get the most from your purchase.

Downloading the example code

You can download the example code files for this book from your account at http://www.packtpub.com. If you purchased this book elsewhere, you can visit http://www.packtpub.com/support and register to have the files emailed directly to you. You can download the code files by following these steps:

1. Log in or register to our website using your email address and password.
2. Hover the mouse pointer on the **SUPPORT** tab at the top.
3. Click on **Code Downloads & Errata**.
4. Enter the name of the book in the **Search** box.
5. Select the book for which you're looking to download the code files.
6. Choose from the drop-down menu where you purchased this book from.
7. Click on **Code Download**.

Once the file is downloaded, please make sure that you unzip or extract the folder using the latest version of:

- WinRAR / 7-Zip for Windows
- Zipeg / iZip / UnRarX for Mac
- 7-Zip / PeaZip for Linux

The code bundle for the book is also hosted on GitHub at https://github.com/PacktPublishing/Statistics-for-Data-Science. We also have other code bundles from our rich catalogue of books and videos available at https://github.com/PacktPublishing/. Check them out!

Downloading the color images of this book

We also provide you with a PDF file that has color images of the screenshots/diagrams used in this book. The color images will help you better understand the changes in the output. You can download this file from https://www.packtpub.com/sites/default/files/downloads/StatisticsforDataScience_ColorImages.pdf.

Errata

Although we have taken every care to ensure the accuracy of our content, mistakes do happen. If you find a mistake in one of our books-maybe a mistake in the text or the code-we would be grateful if you could report this to us. By doing so, you can save other readers from frustration and help us improve subsequent versions of this book. If you find any errata, please report them by visiting http://www.packtpub.com/submit-errata, selecting your book, clicking on the **Errata Submission Form** link, and entering the details of your errata. Once your errata are verified, your submission will be accepted and the errata will be uploaded to our website or added to any list of existing errata under the Errata section of that title. To view the previously submitted errata, go to https://www.packtpub.com/books/content/support and enter the name of the book in the search field. The required information will appear under the **Errata** section.

Piracy

Piracy of copyrighted material on the internet is an ongoing problem across all media. At Packt, we take the protection of our copyright and licenses very seriously. If you come across any illegal copies of our works in any form on the internet, please provide us with the location address or website name immediately so that we can pursue a remedy. Please contact us at copyright@packtpub.com with a link to the suspected pirated material. We appreciate your help in protecting our authors and our ability to bring you valuable content.

Questions

If you have a problem with any aspect of this book, you can contact us at questions@packtpub.com, and we will do our best to address the problem.

1
Transitioning from Data Developer to Data Scientist

In this chapter (and throughout all of the chapters of this book), we will chart your course for starting and continuing the journey from thinking like a data developer to thinking like a data scientist.

Using developer terminologies and analogies, we will discuss a developer's objectives, what a typical developer mindset might be like, how it differs from a data scientist's mindset, why there are important differences (as well as similarities) between the two and suggest how to transition yourself into thinking like a data scientist. Finally, we will suggest certain advantages of understanding statistics and data science, taking a data perspective, as well as simply thinking like a data scientist.

In this chapter, we've broken things into the following topics:

- The objectives of the data developer role
- How a data developer thinks
- The differences between a data developer and a data scientist
- Advantages of thinking like a data scientist
- The steps for transitioning into a data scientist mindset

So, let's get started!

Data developer thinking

Having spent plenty of years wearing the hat of a data developer, it makes sense to start out here with a few quick comments about data developers.

In some circles, a database developer is the equivalent of a data developer. But whether data or database, both would usually be labeled as an **information technology** (**IT**) professional. Both spend their time working on or with data and database technologies.

 We may see a split between those databases (data) developers that focus more on support and routine maintenance (such as administrators) and those who focus more on improving, expanding, and otherwise developing access to data (such as developers).

Your typical data developer will primarily be involved with creating and maintaining access to data rather than consuming that data. He or she will have input in or may make decisions on, choosing programming languages for accessing or manipulating data. We will make sure that new data projects adhere to rules on how databases store and handle data, and we will create interfaces between data sources.

In addition, some data developers are involved with reviewing and tuning queries written by others and, therefore, must be proficient in the latest tuning techniques, various query languages such as **Structured Query Language** (**SQL**), as well as how the data being accessed is stored and structured.

In summary, at least strictly from a data developer's perspective, the focus is all about access to valuable data resources rather than the consumption of those valuable data resources.

Objectives of a data developer

Every role, position, or job post will have its own list of objectives, responsibilities, or initiatives.

As such, in the role of a data developer, one may be charged with some of the following responsibilities:

- Maintaining the integrity of a database and infrastructure
- Monitoring and optimizing to maintain levels of responsiveness
- Ensuring quality and integrity of data resources
- Providing appropriate levels of support to communities of users
- Enforcing security policies on data resources

As a data scientist, you will note somewhat different objectives. This role will typically include some of the objectives listed here:

- Mining data from disparate sources
- Identifying patterns or trending
- Creating statistical models—modeling
- Learning and assessing
- Identifying insights and predicting

Do you perhaps notice a theme beginning here?

Note the keywords:

- Maintaining
- Monitoring
- Ensuring
- Providing
- Enforcing

These terms imply different notions than those terms that may be more associated with the role of a data scientist, such as the following:

- Mining
- Trending
- Modeling
- Learning
- Predicting

There are also, of course, some activities performed that may seem analogous to both a data developer and a data scientist and will be examined here.

Querying or mining

As a data developer, you will almost always be in the habit of querying data. Indeed, a data scientist will query data as well. So, what is data mining? Well, when one queries data, one expects to ask a specific question. For example, you might ask, What was the total number of daffodils sold in April? expecting to receive back a known, relevant answer such as in April, daffodil sales totaled 269 plants.

With data mining, one is usually more absorbed in the data relationships (or the potential relationships between points of data, sometimes referred to as variables) and cognitive analysis. A simple example might be: how does the average daily temperature during the month affect the total number of daffodils sold in April?

Another important distinction between data querying and data mining is that queries are typically historic in nature in that they are used to report past results (total sales in April), while data mining techniques can be forward thinking in that through the use of appropriate statistical methods, they can infer a future result or provide the probability that a result or event will occur. For example, using our earlier example, we might predict higher daffodil sales when the average temperature rises within the selling area.

Data quality or data cleansing

Do you think a data developer is interested in the quality of data in a database? Of course, a data developer needs to care about the level of quality of the data they support or provide access to. For a data developer, the process of **data quality assurance (DQA)** within an organization is more mechanical in nature, such as ensuring data is current and complete and stored in the correct format.

With data cleansing, you see the data scientist put more emphasis on the concept of statistical data quality. This includes using relationships found within the data to improve the levels of data quality. As an example, an individual whose age is nine, should not be labeled or shown as part of a group of legal drivers in the United States incorrectly labeled data.

 You may be familiar with the term **munging data**. Munging may be sometimes defined as the act of tying together systems and interfaces that were not specifically designed to interoperate. Munging can also be defined as the processing or filtering of raw data into another form for a particular use or need.

Data modeling

Data developers create designs (or models) for data by working closely with key stakeholders based on given requirements such as the ability to rapidly enter sales transactions into an organization's online order entry system. During model design, there are three kinds of data models the data developer must be familiar with—conceptual, logical, and physical—each relatively independent of each other.

Data scientists create models with the intention of training with data samples or populations to identify previously unknown insights or validate current assumptions.

Modeling data can become complex, and therefore, it is common to see a distinction between the role of data development and data modeling. In these cases, a data developer concentrates on evaluating the data itself, creating meaningful reports, while data modelers evaluate how to collect, maintain, and use the data.

Issue or insights

A lot of a data developer's time may be spent monitoring data, users, and environments, looking for any indications of emerging issues such as unexpected levels of usage that may cause performance bottlenecks or outages. Other common duties include auditing, application integrations, disaster planning and recovery, capacity planning, change management, database software version updating, load balancing, and so on.

Data scientists spend their time evaluating and analyzing data, and information in an effort to discover valuable new insights. Hopefully, once established, insights can then be used to make better business decisions.

There is a related concept to grasp; through the use of analytics, one can identify patterns and trends within data, while an insight is a value obtained through the use of the analytical outputs.

Thought process

Someone's mental procedures or cognitive activity based on interpretations, past experiences, reasoning, problem-solving, imagining, and decision making make up their way of thinking or their thought process.

One can only guess how particular individuals will actually think, or their exact thoughts at a given point of time or during an activity, or what thought process they will use to accomplish their objectives, but in general terms, a data developer may spend more time thinking about data convenience (making the data available as per the requirements), while data scientists are all about data consumption (concluding new ways to leverage the data to find insights into existing issues or new opportunities).

To paint a clearer picture, you might use the analogy of the auto mechanic and the school counselor.

An auto mechanic will use his skills along with appropriate tools to keep an automobile available to its owner and running well, or if there has been an issue identified with a vehicle, the mechanic will perform diagnosis for the symptoms presented and rectify the problem. This is much like the activities of a data developer.

With a counselor, he or she might examine a vast amount of information regarding a student's past performance, personality traits, as well as economic statistics to determine what opportunities may exist in a particular student's future. In addition, multiple scenarios may be studied to predict what the best outcomes might be, based on this individual student's resources.

Clearly, both aforementioned individuals provide valuable services but use (maybe very) different approaches and individual thought processes to produce the desired results.

Although there is some overlapping, when you are a data developer, your thoughts are normally around maintaining convenient access to appropriate data resources but not particularly around the data's substance, that is, you may care about data types, data volumes, and accessibility paths but not about whether or what cognitive relationships exist or the powerful potential uses for the data.

In the next section, we will explore some simple circumstances in an effort to show various contrasts between the data developer and the data scientist.

Developer versus scientist

To better understand the differences between a data developer and data scientist, let's take a little time here and consider just a few hypotheticals (yet still realistic) situations that may occur during your day.

New data, new source

What happens when new data or a new data source becomes available or is presented?

Here, new data usually means that more **current** or more **up-to-date** data has become available. An example of this might be receiving a file each morning of the latest month-to-date sales transactions, usually referred to as an **actual** update.

 In the business world, data can be either real (actual) as in the case of an authenticated sale, or sale transaction entered in an order processing system, or supposed as in the case of an organization forecasting a future (not yet actually occurred) sale or transaction.

You may receive files of data periodically from an online transactions processing system, which provide the daily sales or sales figures from the first of the month to the current date. You'd want your business reports to show the total sales numbers that include the most recent sales transactions.

The idea of a new data source is different. If we use the same sort of analogy as we used previously, an example of this might be a file of sales transactions from a company that a parent company newly acquired. Perhaps another example would be receiving data reporting the results of a recent online survey. This is the information that's collected with a specific purpose in mind and typically is not (but could be) a routine event.

	New Data	New Data Source
Data Developer	☑	☑
Data Scientist		☑

 Machine (and otherwise) data is accumulating even as you are reading this, providing new and interesting data sources creating a market for data to be consumed. One interesting example might be Amazon Web Services (https://aws.amazon.com/datasets/). Here, you can find massive resources of public data, including the *1000 Genomes Project* (the attempt to build the most comprehensive database of human genetic information) as well as NASA's database of satellite imagery of the Earth.

In the previous scenarios, a data developer would most likely be (should be) expecting updated files and have implemented the **Extract**, **Transform**, and **Load** (**ETL**) processes to automatically process the data, handle any exceptions, and ensure that all the appropriate reports reflect the latest, correct information. Data developers would also deal with transitioning a sales file from a newly acquired company but probably would not be a primary resource for dealing with survey results (or the *1000 Genomes Project*).

Data scientists are not involved in the daily processing of data (such as sales) but will be directly responsible for a survey results project. That is, the data scientist is almost always hands-on with initiatives such as researching and acquiring new sources of information for projects involving surveying. Data scientists most likely would have input even in the designing of surveys as they are the ones who will be using that data in their analysis.

Quality questions

Suppose there are concerns about the quality of the data to be, or being, consumed by the organization. As we eluded to earlier in this chapter, there are different types of data quality concerns such as what we called **mechanical issues** as well as **statistical issues** (and there are others).

 Current trending examples of the most common statistical quality concerns include duplicate entries and misspellings, misclassification and aggregation, and changing meanings.

If management is questioning the validity of the total sales listed on a daily report or perhaps doesn't trust it because the majority of your customers are not legally able to drive in the United States, the number of the organizations repeat customers are declining, you have a quality issue:

	Data Quality
Data Developer	☑
Data Scientist	☑

Quality is a concern to both the data developer and the data scientist. A data developer focuses more on timing and formatting (the mechanics of the data), while the data scientist is more interested in the data's statistical quality (with priority given to issues with the data that may potentially impact the reliability of a particular study).

Querying and mining

Historically, the information technology group or department has been beseeched by a variety of business users to produce and provide reports showing information stored in databases and systems that are of interest.

These ad hoc reporting requests have evolved into requests for on-demand raw data extracts (rather than formatted or pretty printed reports) so that business users could then import the extracted data into a tool such as MS Excel (or others), where they could then perform their own formatting and reporting, or perform further analysis and modeling. In today's world, business users demand more self-service (even mobile) abilities to meet their organization's (or an individual's) analytical and reporting needs, expecting to have access to the updated raw data stores, directly or through smaller, focus-oriented data pools.

If business applications cannot supply the necessary reporting on their own, business users often will continue their self-service journey.

-Christina Wong

(www.datainformed.com)

	Query	Mining
Data Developer	☑	
Data Scientist	☑	☑

Creating ad hoc reports and performing extracts based on specific on-demand needs or providing self-service access to data falls solely to the role of the organization's data developer. However, take note that a data scientist will want to periodically perform his or her own querying and extracting—usually as part of a project they are working on. They may use these query results to determine the viability and availability of the data they need or as part of the process to create a sampling or population for specific statistical projects. This form of querying may be considered to be a form of data mining and goes much deeper into the data than queries might. This work effort is typically performed by a data scientist rather than a data developer.

Performance

You can bet that pretty much everyone is, or will be, concerned with the topic of performance. Some forms (of performance) are perhaps a bit more quantifiable, such as what is an acceptable response time for an ad hoc query or extract to complete? Or perhaps what are the total number of mouse-clicks or keystrokes required to enter a sales order? Others may be a bit more difficult to answer or address, such as why does it appear that there is a downward trend in the number of repeat customers?

	Performance
Data Developer	☑
Data Scientist	☑

It is the responsibility of the data developer to create and support data designs (even be involved with infrastructure configuration options) that consistently produce swift response times and are easy to understand and use.

One area of performance responsibility that may be confusing is in the area of website performance. For example, if an organization's website is underperforming, is it because certain pages are slow to load or uninteresting and/or irrelevant to the targeted audience or customer? In this example, both a data developer and a data scientist may be directed to address the problem.

These individuals—data developers—would not play a part in survey projects. The data scientist, on the other hand, will not be included in day-to-day transactional (or similar) performance concerns but would be the key responsible person to work with the organization's stakeholders by defining and leading a statistical project in an effort to answer a question such as the one concerning repeat-customer counts.

Financial reporting

In every organization, there is a need to produce regular financial statements (such as an Income Statement, Balance Sheet, or Cash Flow statement). Financial reporting (or Fin reporting) is looking to answer key questions regarding the business, such as the following:

- Are we making a profit or losing money?
- How do assets compare to liabilities?
- How much free cash do we have or need?

The process of creating, updating, and validating regular financial statements is a mandatory task for any business—profit or non-profit based—of just about any size, whether public or private. Organizations, still today, are not all using fully automated reporting solutions. This means that even the task of updating a single report with the latest data could be a daunting ordeal.

	Financial Reporting
Data Developer	☑
Data Scientist	

Financial reporting is one area that is (pretty) clearly defined within the industry as far as responsibilities go. A data developer would be the one to create and support the processing and systems that make the data available, ensure its correctness, and even (in some cases) create and distribute reports.

Over 83 percent of businesses in the world today utilize MS Excel for Month End close and reporting

`-https://`
`venasolutions.com/`

Typically, a data developer would work to provide and maintain the data to feed these efforts.

Data scientists typically do not support an organization's routine processing and (financial) reporting efforts. A data scientist would, however, perform analysis of the produced financial information (and supporting data) to produce reports and visualizations indicating insights around management performance in profitability, efficiency, and risk (to name a few).

One particularly interesting area of statistics and data science is when a data scientist performs a vertical analysis to identify relationships of variables to a base amount within an organization's financial statement.

Visualizing

It is a common practice today to produce visualizations in a dashboard format that can show updated individual **key performance indicators (KPI)**. Moreover, communicating a particular point or simplifying the complexities of mountains of data does not require the use of data visualization techniques, but in some ways, today's world may demand it.

	Visualization
Data Developer	☑
Data Scientist	☑

Most would likely agree that scanning numerous worksheets, spreadsheets, or reports is mundane and tedious at best while looking at charts and graphs (such as a visualization) is typically much easier on the eyes. To that point, both the data developer and the data scientist will equally be found designing, creating, and using data visualizations. The difference will be found in the types of visualizations being created. Data developers usually focus on the visualization of repetitive data points (forecast versus actuals, to name a common example), while data scientists use visualizations to make a point as part of a statistical project.

Again, a data developer most likely will leverage visualizations to illustrate or highlight, for example, sales volumes, month-to-month for the year, while a data scientist may use visualizations to predict potential sales volumes, month-to-month for next year, given seasonality (and other) statistics.

Tools of the trade

The tools and technologies used by individuals to access and consume data can vary significantly depending upon an assortment of factors such as the following:

- The type of business
- The type of business problem (or opportunity)
- Security or legal requirements
- Hardware and software compatibilities and/or perquisites
- The type and use of data
- The specifics around the user communities
- Corporate policies
- Price

	Tools of the Trade
Data Developer	☑
Data Scientist	☑

In an ever-changing technology climate, the data developer and data scientist have ever more, and perhaps overwhelming, choices including very viable open source options.

 Open source software is software developed by and for the user community. The good news is that open source software is used in the vast majority, or 78 percent, of worldwide businesses today—Vaughan-Nichols, http://www.zdnet.com/. Open source is playing a continually important role in data science.

When we talk about tools and technologies, both the data developer and the data scientist will be equally involved in choosing the correct tool or technology that best fits their individual likes and dislikes and meets the requirements of the project or objective.

Advantages of thinking like a data scientist

So why should you, a data developer, endeavor to think like (or more like) a data scientist? What is the significance of gaining an understanding of the ways and how's of statistics? Specifically, what might be the advantages of thinking like a data scientist?

The following are just a few notions supporting the effort for making the move into data science:

- Developing a better approach to understanding data
- Using statistical thinking during the process of program or database designing
- Adding to your personal toolbox
- Increased marketability
- Perpetual learning
- Seeing the future

Developing a better approach to understanding data

Whether you are a data developer, systems analyst, programmer/developer, or data scientist, or other business or technology professional, you need to be able to develop a comprehensive relationship with the data you are working with or designing an application or database schema for.

Some might rely on the data specifications provided to you as part of the overall project plan or requirements, and still, some (usually those with more experience) may supplement their understanding by performing some generic queries on the data, either way, this seldom is enough.

In fact, in industry case studies, unclear, misunderstood, or incomplete requirements or specifications consistently rank in the top five as reasons for project failure or added risk.

Profiling data is a process, characteristic of data science, aimed at establishing data intimacy (or a more clear and concise grasp of the data and its inward relationships). Profiling data also establishes context to which there are several general contextual categories, which can be used to augment or increase the value and understanding of data for any purpose or project.

These categories include the following:

- **Definitions and explanations**: These help gain additional information or attributes about data points within your data
- **Comparisons**: This help add a comparable value to a data point within your data
- **Contrasts**: This help add an opposite to a data point to see whether it perhaps determines a different perspective
- **Tendencies**: These are typical mathematical calculations, summaries, or aggregations
- **Dispersion**: This includes mathematical calculations (or summaries) such as range, variance, and standard deviation, describing the average of a dataset (or group within the data)

 Think of data profiling as the process you may have used for examining data in a data file and collecting statistics and information about that data. Those statistics most likely drove the logic implemented in a program or how you related data in tables of a database.

Using statistical thinking during program or database designing

The process of creating a database design commonly involves several tasks that will be carried out by the database designer (or data developer). Usually, the designer will perform the following:

1. Identify what data will be kept in the database.
2. Establish the relationships between the different data points.
3. Create a logical data structure to be used on the basis of steps 1 and 2.

Even during the act of application program designing, a thorough understanding of how the data works is essential. Without understanding average or default values, relationships between data points and grouping, and so on, the created application is at risk of failing.

One idea for applying statistical thinking to help with data designing is in the case where there is limited real data available. If enough data cannot be collected, one could create sample (test) data by a variety of sampling methods, such as probability sampling.

A probability-based sample is created by constructing a list of the target population values, called a **sample frame**, then a randomized process for selecting records from the sample frame, which is called a **selection procedure**. Think of this as creating a script to generate records of sample data based on your knowledge of actual data as well as some statistical logic to be used for testing your designs.

Finally, approach any problem with scientific or statistical methods, and odds are you'll produce better results.

Adding to your personal toolbox

In my experience, most data developers tend to lock on to a technology or tool based upon a variety of factors (some of which we mentioned earlier in this chapter) becoming increasingly familiar with and (hopefully) more proficient with the product, tool, or technology—even the continuously released newer versions. One might suspect that (and probably would be correct) the more the developer uses the tool, the higher the skill level that he or she establishes. Data scientists, however, seem to lock onto methodologies, practices, or concepts more than the actual tools and technologies they use to implement them.

This turning of focus (from to tool to technique) changes one's mindset to the idea of thinking what tool best serves my objective rather than how this tool serves my objective.

The more tools you are exposed to, the broader your thinking will become a developer or data scientist. The open source community provides outstanding tools you can download, learn, and use freely. One should adopt a mindset of what's next or new to learn, even if it's in an attempt to compare features and functions of a new tool to your preferred tool. We'll talk more about this in the perpetual learning section of this chapter.

An exciting example of a currently popular data developer or data enabling tool is **MarkLogic** (`http://www.marklogic.com/`). This is an operational and transactional enterprise NoSQL database that is designed to integrate, store, manage, and search more data than ever before. MarkLogic received the 2017 DAVIES Award for best Data Development Tools. R and Python seem to be at the top as options for the data scientists.

It would not be appropriate to end this section without the mention of IBM Watson Analytics (`https://www.ibm.com/watson/`), currently transforming the way the industry thinks about statistical or cognitive thinking.

Increased marketability

Data science is clearly an ever-evolving field, with exponentially growing popularity. In fact, I'd guess that if you ask a dozen professionals, you'll most likely receive a dozen different definitions of what a data scientist is (and their place within a project or organization), but most likely, all would agree with their level of importance and that vast numbers of opportunities exist within the industry and the world today.

> *Data scientist face an unprecedented demand for more models, more insights...there's only one way to do that: They have to dramatically speed up the insights to action. In the future data Scientists, must become more productive. That's the only way they're going to get more value from the data.*
>
> *-Gualtieri*
>
> `https://www.datanami.com/2015/09/18/the-future-of-data-science/`

Data Scientist is relatively hard to find today. If you do your research, you will find that today's data scientists may have a mixed background consisting of mathematics, programming, and software design, experimental design, engineering, communication, and management skills. In practice, you'll see that most data scientists you find aren't specialists in any one aspect, rather they possess varying levels of proficiency in several areas or backgrounds.

> *The role of the data scientist has unequivocally evolved since the field of statistics of over 1200 years ago. Despite the term only existing since the turn of this century, it has already been labeled The Sexiest Job of the 21st Century, which understandably, has created a queue of applicants stretched around the block*
>
> *-Pearson*
>
> `https://www.linkedin.com/pulse/evolution-data-scientist-chris-pearson`

Currently, there is no official data scientist job description (or prerequisite list for that matter). This presents you with the opportunity to create your own flavour of the data scientist, delivering value in new ways to your organization.

Perpetual learning

The idea of continued assessment or perpetual learning is an important statistical concept to grasp. Consider learning enhanced skills of perception as a common definition. For example, in statistics, we can refer to the idea of cross-validation. This is a statistical approach for measuring (assessing) a statistical model's performance. This practice involves identifying a set of validation values and then running a model a set number of rounds (continuously), using sample datasets and then averaging the results of each round to ultimately see how good a model (or approach) might be in solving a particular problem or meeting an objective.

The expectation here is that given performance results, adjustments could be made to tweak the model so as to provide the ability to identify insights when used with a real or full population of data. Not only is this concept a practice the data developer should use for refining or fine-tuning a data design or data-driven application process, but this is great life advice in the form of try, learn, adjust, and repeat.

The idea of model assessment is not unique to statistics. Data developers might consider this similar to the act of predicting SQL performance or perhaps the practice of an application walkthrough where an application is validated against the intent and purpose stated within its documented requirements.

Seeing the future

Predictive modeling uses the statistics of data science to predict or foresee a result (actually, a probable result). This may sound a lot like fortune telling, but it is more about putting to use cognitive reasoning to interpret information (mined from data) to draw a conclusion. In the way that a scientist might be described as someone who acts in a methodical way, attempting to obtain knowledge or to learn, a data scientist might be thought of as trying to make predictions, using statistics and (machine) learning.

When we talk about predicting a result, it's really all about the probability of seeing a certain result. Probability deals with predicting the likelihood of future events, while statistics involves the analysis of the frequency of past events.

If you are a data developer who has perhaps worked on projects serving an organization's office of finance, you may understand why a business leader would find it of value to not just report on its financial results (even the most accurate of results are really still historical events) but also to be able to make educated assumptions on future performance.

Perhaps you can understand that if you have a background in and are responsible for financial reporting, you can now take the step towards providing statistical predictions to those reports!

 Statistical modeling techniques can also be applied to any type of unknown event, regardless of when it occurred, such as in the case of crime detection and suspect identification.

Transitioning to a data scientist

Let's start this section by taking a moment to state what I consider to be a few generally accepted facts about transitioning to a data scientist. We'll reaffirm these beliefs as we continue through this book:

- Academia: Data scientists are not all from one academic background. They are not all computer science or statistics/mathematics majors. They do not all possess an advanced degree (in fact, you can use statistics and data science with a bachelor's degree or even less).
- It's not magic-based: Data scientists can use machine learning and other accepted statistical methods to identify insights from data, not magic.
- They are not all tech or computer geeks: You don't need years of programming experience or expensive statistical software to be effective.
- You don't need to be experienced to get started. You can start today, right now. (Well, you already did when you bought this book!)

Okay, having made the previous declarations, let's also be realistic. As always, there is an entry-point for everything in life, and, to give credit where it is due, the more credentials you can acquire to begin out with, the better off you will most likely be. Nonetheless, (as we'll see later in this chapter), there is absolutely no valid reason why you cannot begin understanding, using, and being productive with data science and statistics immediately.

 As with any profession, certifications, and degrees carry the weight that may open the doors, while experience, as always, might be considered the best teacher. There are, however, no fake data scientists but only those with currently more desire than practical experience.

If you are seriously interested in not only understanding statistics and data science but eventually working as a full-time data scientist, you should consider the following common themes (you're likely to find in job postings for data scientists) as areas to focus on:

- **Education**: Common fields of study are Mathematics and Statistics, followed by Computer Science and Engineering (also Economics and Operations research). Once more, there is no strict requirement to have an advanced or even related degree. In addition, typically, the idea of a degree or an equivalent experience will also apply here.
- **Technology**: You will hear SAS and R (actually, you will hear quite a lot about R) as well as Python, Hadoop, and SQL mentioned as key or preferable for a data scientist to be comfortable with, but tools and technologies change all the time so, as mentioned several times throughout this chapter, data developers can begin to be productive as soon as they understand the objectives of data science and various statistical mythologies without having to learn a new tool or language.

Basic business skills such as Omniture, Google Analytics, SPSS, Excel, or any other Microsoft Office tool are assumed pretty much everywhere and don't really count as an advantage, but experience with programming languages (such as Java, PERL, or C++) or databases (such as MySQL, NoSQL, Oracle, and so on.) does help!

- **Data**: The ability to understand data and deal with the challenges specific to the various types of data, such as unstructured, machine-generated, and big data (including organizing and structuring large datasets).

Unstructured data is a key area of interest in statistics and for a data scientist. It is usually described as data having no redefined model defined for it or is not organized in a predefined manner. Unstructured information is characteristically text-heavy but may also contain dates, numbers, and various other facts as well.

- **Intellectual curiosity**: I love this. This is perhaps well defined as a character trait that comes in handy (if not required) if you want to be a data scientist. This means that you have a continuing need to know more than the basics or want to go beyond the common knowledge about a topic (you don't need a degree on the wall for this!)
- **Business acumen**: To be a data developer or a data scientist you need a deep understanding of the industry you're working in, and you also need to know what business problems your organization needs to unravel. In terms of data science, being able to discern which problems are the most important to solve is critical in addition to identifying new ways the business should be leveraging its data.

- **Communication skills**: All companies look for individuals who can clearly and fluently translate their findings to a non-technical team, such as the marketing or sales departments. As a data scientist, one must be able to enable the business to make decisions by arming them with quantified insights in addition to understanding the needs of their non-technical colleagues to add value and be successful.

Let's move ahead

So, let's finish up this chapter with some casual (if not common sense) advice for the data developer who wants to learn statistics and transition into the world of data science.

Following are several recommendations you should consider to be resources for familiarizing yourself with the topic of statistics and data science:

- **Books**: Still the best way to learn! You can get very practical and detailed information (with examples) and advice from books. It's great you started with this book, but there is literally a staggering amount (and growing all the time) of written resources just waiting for you to consume.
- **Google**: I'm a big fan of doing internet research. You will be surprised at the quantity and quality of open source and otherwise, free software libraries, utilities, models, sample data, white papers, blogs, and so on you can find out there. A lot of it can be downloaded and used directly to educate you or even as part of an actual project or deliverable.
- **LinkedIn**: A very large percentage of corporate and independent recruiters use social media, and most use LinkedIn. This is an opportunity to see what types of positions are in demand and exactly what skills and experiences they require. When you see something you don't recognize, do the research to educate yourself on the topic. In addition, LinkedIn has an enormous number of groups that focus on statistics and data science. Join them all! Network with the members--even ask them direct questions. For the most part, the community is happy to help you (even if it's only to show how much they know).
- **Volunteer:** A great way to build skills, continue learning, and expand your statistics network is to volunteer. Check out http://www.datakind.org/get-involved. If you sign up to volunteer, they will review your skills and keep in touch with projects that are a fit for your background or you are interested in coming up.

- **Internship**: Experienced professionals may re-enlist as interns to test a new profession or break into a new industry (www.Wetfeet.com). Although perhaps unrealistic for anyone other than a recent college graduate, internships are available if you can afford to cut your pay (or even take no pay) for a period of time to gain some practical experience in statistics and data science. What might be more practical is interning within your own company as a data scientist apprentice role for a short period or for a particular project.

- **Side projects**: This is one of my favorites. Look for opportunities within your organization where statistics may be in use, and ask to sit in meetings or join calls in your own time. If that isn't possible, look for scenarios where statistics and data science might solve a problem or address an issue, and make it a pet project you work on in your spare time. These kinds of projects are low risk as there will be no deadlines, and if they don't work out at first, it's not the end of the world.

- **Data**: Probably one of the easiest things you can do to help your transition into statistics and data science is to get your hands on more types of data, especially unstructured data and big data. Additionally, it's always helpful to explore data from other industries or applications.

- **Coursera** and **Kaggle**: Coursera is an online website where you can take **Massive Online Open Curriculum** (**MOOCs**) courses for a fee and earn a certification, while Kaggle hosts data science contests where you can not only evaluate your abilities as you transition against other members but also get access to large, unstructured big data files that may be more like the ones you might use on an actual statistical project.

- **Diversify:** To add credibility to your analytic skills (since many companies are adopting numerous arrays of new tools every day) such as R, Python, SAS, Scala, (of course) SQL, and so on, you will have a significant advantage if you spend time acquiring knowledge in as many tools and technologies as you can. In addition to those mainstream data science tools, you may want to investigate some of the up-and-comers such as Paxada, MatLab, Trifacta, Google Cloud Prediction API, or Logical Glue.

- **Ask a recruiter**: Taking the time to develop a relationship with a recruiter early in your transformation will provide many advantages, but a trusted recruiter can pass on a list of skills that are currently in demand as well as which statistical practices are most popular. In addition, as you gain experience and confidence, a recruiter can help you focus or fine-tune your experiences towards specific opportunities that may be further out on the horizon, potentially giving you an advantage over other candidates.

- **Online videos**: Check out webinars and how to videos on YouTube. There are endless resources from both amateurs and professionals that you can view whenever your schedule allows.

Summary

In this chapter, we sketched how a database (or data) developer thinks on a day-to-day, problem-solving basis, comparing the mindsets of a data developer and a data scientist, using various practical examples.

We also listed some of the advantages of thinking as a data scientist and finally discussed common themes for you to focus on as you gain an understanding of statistics and transition into the world of data science.

In the next chapter, we will introduce and explain (again, from a developer's perspective) the basic objectives behind statistics for data science and introduce you to the important terms and key concepts (with easily understood explanations and examples) that are used throughout the book.

2
Declaring the Objectives

This chapter introduces and explains (yet again, from a developer's perspective) the basic objectives behind statistics for data science and introduces the reader to the important terms and key concepts (with explanations and examples) that are used throughout the book.

In this chapter, we've broken things down into the following topics:

- A primer on the key objectives of data science
- Bringing statistics into data science
- Common terminologies used with statistics and data science

Key objectives of data science

As mentioned in Chapter 1, *Transitioning from Data Developer to Data Scientist*, the idea of how data science is defined is a matter of opinion.

I personally like the explanation that data science is a progression or, even better, an evolution of thought or steps, as shown in the following figure:

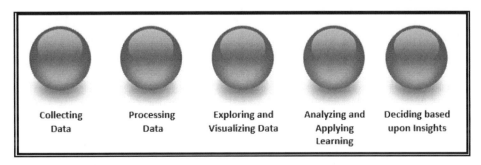

This data science evolution (depicted in the preceding figure) consists of a series of steps or phases that a data scientist tracks, comprising the following:

- Collecting data
- Processing data
- Exploring and visualizing data
- Analyzing (data) and/or applying machine learning (to data)
- Deciding (or planning) based on acquired insight

Although a progression or evolution implies a sequential journey, in practice, this is an extremely fluid process; each of the phases may inspire the data scientist to reverse and repeat one or more of the phases until they are satisfied. In other words, all or some phases of the process may be repeated until the data scientist determines that the desired outcome is reached.

For example, after a careful review of a generated visualization (during the *Exploring and visualizing data* phase), one may determine that additional processing of the data is required or that additional data needs to be collected before any reasonable analysis or learning could be of value.

 You might loosely compare the data science process to the agile software development mythology where a developer performs various tasks, the results are analyzed, more work is done, the work is again reviewed, and the process is repeated until the desired results or outcomes are obtained.

Let's explain each of the phases of the data science evolution.

Collecting data

This should be somewhat obvious—without (at least some) data, we cannot perform any of the subsequent steps (although one might argue the point of inference, that would be inappropriate. There is no magic in data science. We, as data scientists, don't make something from anything. Inference (which we'll define later in this chapter) requires at least some data to begin with.

Some new concepts for collecting data include the fact that data can be collected from ample of sources, and the number and types of data sources continue to grow daily. In addition, how data is collected might require a perspective new to a data developer; data for data science isn't always sourced from a relational database, rather from machine-generated logging files, online surveys, performance statistics, and so on; again, the list is ever evolving.

Another point to ponder—collecting data also involves supplementation. For example, a data scientist might determine that he or she needs to be adding additional demographics to a particular pool of application data previously collected, processed, and reviewed.

Processing data

The processing (or transformation) of data is where the data scientist's programming skills will come in to play (although you can often find a data scientist performing some sort of processing in other steps, like collecting, visualizing, or learning).

Keep in mind that there are many aspects of processing that occur within data science. The most common are formatting (and reformatting), which involves activities such as mechanically setting data types, aggregating values, reordering or dropping columns, and so on, cleansing (or addressing the quality of the data), which is solving for such things as default or missing values, incomplete or inapposite values, and so on, and profiling, which adds context to the data by creating a statistical understanding of the data.

The processing to be completed on the data can be simple (for example, it can be a very simple and manual event requiring repetitious updates to data in an MS Excel worksheet), or complex (as with the use of programming languages such as R or Python), or even more sophisticated (as when processing logic is coded into routines that can then be scheduled and rerun automatically on new populations of data).

Exploring and visualizing data

During this phase or step in the overall data science pipeline process, the data scientist will use various methods to dig deeper into the data. Typically, several graphical representations are created (again, either manually or through a programming script or tool) emphasizing or validating a data scientist's observation, a particular point, or belief. This is a significant step in the overall data science process as the data scientist may come to understand that additional processing should be done on the data, or additional data needs to be collected, or perhaps the original theories appear to be validated. These findings will be cause for a pause, reflecting on the next steps that need to be taken. Should the data scientist proceed with the formal analysis process, perhaps creating a predictive model for automated learning? Or, should the scientist revisit a previous step, collecting additional (or different) data for processing?

Data visualization is a key technique permitting data scientists to perform analyses, identify key trends or events, and make more confident decisions much more quickly.

Analyzing the data and/or applying machine learning to the data

In this phase, quite a bit of analysis takes place as the data scientist (driven by a high level of scientific curiosity and experience) attempts to shape a story based upon an observation or the interpretation of their understanding of the data (up to this point). The data scientist continues to slice and dice the data, using analytics or BI packages—such as Tableau or Pentaho or an open source solution such as R or Python—to create a concrete data storyline. Once again, based on these analysis results, the data scientist may elect to again go back to a prior phase, pulling new data, processing and reprocessing, and creating additional visualizations. At some point, when appropriate progress has been made, the data scientist may decide that the data is at such point where data analysis can begin. Machine learning (defined further later in this chapter) has evolved over time from being more of an exercise in pattern recognition to now being defined as utilizing a selected statistical method to dig deeper, using the data and results of the analysis of this phase to learn and make a prediction, on the project data.

The ability of a data scientist to extract a quantitative result from data through machine learning and express it as something that everyone (not just other data scientists) can understand immediately is an invaluable skill, and we will talk more about this throughout this book.

Deciding (or planning) based upon acquired insight

In this step, the data scientist hopes to obtain value from their efforts in the form of an insight. The insight is gained by performing the preceding described phases, aimed at gaining an understanding of a particular situation or phenomena. The idea is that this insight can then be used as input to make better decisions.

A fun example that illustrates a creative use of insights mined from data is the (as of this writing, experimental) Roztayger personality match process powered by IBM Watson. Using either your Facebook or Twitter feeds (or you can enter a short bio), Watson will, on-the-fly, perform an analysis of your personality. The results are interesting and pretty spot on, and these insights are then used to suggest designer labels that may best suit you and your personal style.

 You can find this feature at `http://roztayger.com/match`. The Personality Insights service extracts personality characteristics based on how a person writes. You can use the service to match individuals to other individuals, opportunities, and products, or tailor their experience with personalized messaging and recommendations. Characteristics include the Big 5 Personality Traits, Values, and Needs. At least 1,200 words of input text are recommended when using this service.

Once the (real-time) data science analysis is complete, the aforementioned website not only provides its recommendations but also shares the data behind its insights, showing an easy-to-understand, well-organized tabular view of the results, and an eye-catching visualization as well, as shown in the following figure:

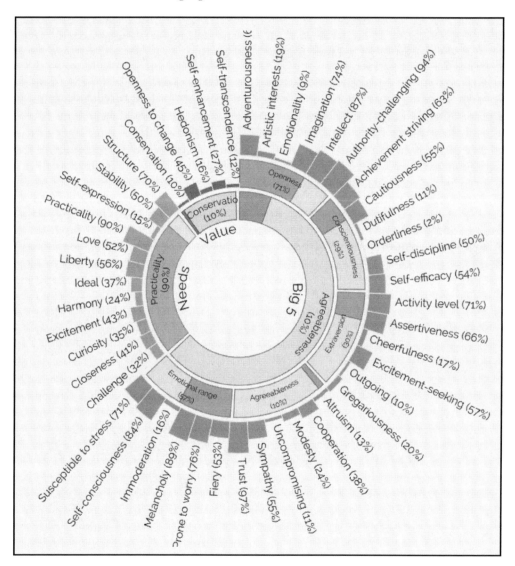

This illustrates another key aspect of this phase of the data science progression, that is, once the data scientist identifies an insight, he must clearly present and communicate those data insights/findings.

Thinking like a data scientist

As we've already stressed, agreement on the concepts of what a data scientist is and does are still just emerging. The entire field of data science is at best roughly defined. Transitioning to data science is perhaps as much about finding an organization or group whose needs match your skills as it is about understanding what skills and concepts are involved in data science and then working towards developing those skills.

 Just as a data developer stays up to date and knowledgeable on the trends and tools in and around the manipulation of and access to data, so should the would-be data scientist.

Bringing statistics into data science

Depending on your sources and individual beliefs, you may say the following:

Statistics is data science, and data science is statistics.

To clarify this, note that there is a popular opinion that statistics might be thought of as a study or process that covers the collection, analysis, interpretation, presentation, and organization of data. As you can see, that definition is pretty similar to the data science process we described in the previous section of this chapter.

Digging deeper into this topic, one will find that statistics always involves (or a collection of) techniques or approaches used to help analyze and present data (again, this understanding could also be used to describe data science).

 It is commonly accepted that the terms data science and statistics have the same meaning, at least within some circles. Again, alignment of terms and concepts is still evolving among data scientists.

Common terminology

Based upon personal experience, research, and various industry experts' advice, someone delving into the art of data science should take every opportunity to understand and gain experience as well as proficiency with the following list of common data science terms:

- Statistical population
- Probability
- False positives
- Statistical inference
- Regression
- Fitting
- Categorical data
- Classification
- Clustering
- Statistical comparison
- Coding
- Distributions
- Data mining
- Decision trees
- Machine learning
- Munging and wrangling
- Visualization
- D3
- Regularization
- Assessment
- Cross-validation
- Neural networks
- Boosting
- Lift
- Mode
- Outlier
- Predictive modeling
- Big data
- Confidence interval
- Writing

Statistical population

You can perhaps think of a statistical population as a recordset (or a set of records). This set or group of records will be of similar items or events that are of interest to the data scientist for some experiment.

For a data developer, a population of data may be a recordset of all sales transactions for a month, and the interest might be reporting to the senior management of an organization which products are the fastest sellers and at which time of the year.

For a data scientist, a population may be a recordset of all emergency room admissions during a month, and the area of interest might be to determine the statistical demographics for emergency room use.

 Typically, the terms **statistical population** and **statistical model** are or can be used interchangeably. Once again, data scientists continue to evolve with their alignment on their use of common terms.

Another key point concerning statistical populations is that the recordset may be a group of (actually) existing objects or a hypothetical group of objects. Using the preceding example, you might draw a comparison of actual objects as those actual sales transactions recorded for the month while the hypothetical objects as sales transactions are expected, forecast, or presumed (based upon observations or experienced assumptions or other logic) to occur during a month.

Finally, through the use of statistical inference (explained later in this chapter), the data scientist can select a portion or subset of the recordset (or population) with the intention that it will represent the total population for a particular area of interest. This subset is known as a **statistical sample**.

If a sample of a population is chosen accurately, characteristics of the entire population (that the sample is drawn from) can be estimated from the corresponding characteristics of the sample.

Probability

> *Probability is concerned with the laws governing random events.*
> *-www.britannica.com*

When thinking of probability, you think of possible upcoming events and the likelihood of them actually occurring. This compares to a statistical thought process that involves analyzing the frequency of past events in an attempt to explain or make sense of the observations. In addition, the data scientist will associate various individual events, studying the relationship of these events. How these different events relate to each other governs the methods and rules that will need to be followed when we're studying their probabilities.

 A probability distribution is a table that is used to show the probabilities of various outcomes in a sample population or recordset.

False positives

The idea of false positives is a very important statistical (data science) concept. A false positive is a mistake or an errored result. That is, it is a scenario where the results of a process or experiment indicate a fulfilled or true condition when, in fact, the condition is not true (not fulfilled). This situation is also referred to by some data scientists as a false alarm and is most easily understood by considering the idea of a recordset or statistical population (which we discussed earlier in this section) that is determined not only by the accuracy of the processing but by the characteristics of the sampled population. In other words, the data scientist has made errors during the statistical process, or the recordset is a population that does not have an appropriate sample (or characteristics) for what is being investigated.

Statistical inference

What developer at some point in his or her career, had to create a sample or test data? For example, I've often created a simple script to generate a random number (based upon the number of possible options or choices) and then used that number as the selected option (in my test recordset). This might work well for data development, but with statistics and data science, this is not sufficient.

To create sample data (or a sample population), the data scientist will use a process called **statistical inference**, which is the process of deducing options of an underlying distribution through analysis of the data you have or are trying to generate for. The process is sometimes called **inferential statistical analysis** and includes testing various hypotheses and deriving estimates.

When the data scientist determines that a recordset (or population) should be larger than it actually is, it is assumed that the recordset is a sample from a larger population, and the data scientist will then utilize statistical inference to make up the difference.

The data or recordset in use is referred to by the data scientist as the observed data. Inferential statistics can be contrasted with descriptive statistics, which is only concerned with the properties of the observed data and does not assume that the recordset came from a larger population.

Regression

Regression is a process or method (selected by the data scientist as the best fit technique for the experiment at hand) used for determining the relationships among variables. If you're a programmer, you have a certain understanding of what a variable is, but in statistics, we use the term differently. Variables are determined to be either dependent or independent.

An independent variable (also known as a **predictor**) is the one that is manipulated by the data scientist in an effort to determine its relationship with a dependent variable. A dependent variable is a variable that the data scientist is measuring.

It is not uncommon to have more than one independent variable in a data science progression or experiment.

More precisely, regression is the process that helps the data scientist comprehend how the typical value of the dependent variable (or criterion variable) changes when any one or more of the independent variables is varied while the other independent variables are held fixed.

Fitting

Fitting is the process of measuring how well a statistical model or process describes a data scientist's observations pertaining to a recordset or experiment. These measures will attempt to point out the discrepancy between observed values and probable values. The probable values of a model or process are known as a distribution or a probability distribution.

Therefore, a probability distribution fitting (or distribution fitting) is when the data scientist fits a probability distribution to a series of data concerning the repeated measurement of a variable phenomenon.

The object of a data scientist performing a distribution fitting is to predict the probability or to forecast the frequency of, the occurrence of the phenomenon at a certain interval.

 One of the most common uses of fitting is to test whether two samples are drawn from identical distributions.

There are numerous probability distributions a data scientist can select from. Some will fit better to the observed frequency of the data than others will. The distribution giving a close fit is supposed to lead to good predictions; therefore, the data scientist needs to select a distribution that suits the data well.

Categorical data

Earlier, we explained how variables in your data can be either independent or dependent. Another type of variable definition is a categorical variable. This type of variable is one that can take on one of a limited, and typically fixed, number of possible values, thus assigning each individual to a particular category.

Often, the collected data's meaning is unclear. Categorical data is a method that a data scientist can use to put meaning to the data.

For example, if a numeric variable is collected (let's say the values found are 4, 10, and 12), the meaning of the variable becomes clear if the values are categorized. Let's suppose that based upon an analysis of how the data was collected, we can group (or categorize) the data by indicating that this data describes university students, and there is the following number of players:

- 4 tennis players
- 10 soccer players
- 12 football players

Now, because we grouped the data into categories, the meaning becomes clear.

Some other examples of categorized data might be individual pet preferences (grouped by the type of pet), or vehicle ownership (grouped by the style of a car owned), and so on.

So, categorical data, as the name suggests, is data grouped into some sort of category or multiple categories. Some data scientists refer to categories as sub-populations of data.

Categorical data can also be data that is collected as a yes or no answer. For example, hospital admittance data may indicate that patients either smoke or do not smoke.

Classification

Statistical classification of data is the process of identifying which category (discussed in the previous section) a data point, observation, or variable should be grouped into. The data science process that carries out a classification process is known as a **classifier**.

 Determining whether a book is fiction or non-fiction is a simple example classification. An analysis of data about restaurants might lead to the classification of them among several genres.

Clustering

Clustering is the process of dividing up the data occurrences into groups or homogeneous subsets of the dataset, not a predetermined set of groups as in classification (described in the preceding section) but groups identified by the execution of the data science process based upon similarities that it found among the occurrences.

Objects in the same group (a group is also referred to as a cluster) are found to be more analogous (in some sense or another) to each other than to those objects found in other groups (or found in other clusters). The process of clustering is found to be very common in exploratory data mining and is also a common technique for statistical data analysis.

Statistical comparison

Simply put, when you hear the term statistical comparison, one is usually referring to the act of a data scientist performing a process of analysis to view the similarities or variances of two or more groups or populations (or recordsets).

As a data developer, one might be familiar with various utilities such as FC Compare, UltraCompare, or WinDiff, which aim to provide the developer with a line-by-line comparison of the contents of two or more (even binary) files.

In statistics (data science), this process of comparing is a statistical technique to compare populations or recordsets. In this method, a data scientist will conduct what is called an **Analysis of Variance (ANOVA)**, compare categorical variables (within the recordsets), and so on.

ANOVA is an assortment of statistical methods that are used to analyze the differences among group means and their associated procedures (such as variations among and between groups, populations, or recordsets). This method eventually evolved into the Six Sigma dataset comparisons.

Coding

Coding or statistical coding is again a process that a data scientist will use to prepare data for analysis. In this process, both quantitative data values (such as income or years of education) and qualitative data (such as race or gender) are categorized or coded in a consistent way.

Coding is performed by a data scientist for various reasons such as follows:

- More effective for running statistical models
- Computers understand the variables
- Accountability--so the data scientist can run models blind, or without knowing what variables stand for, to reduce programming/author bias

 You can imagine the process of coding as the means to transform data into a form required for a system or application.

Distributions

The distribution of a statistical recordset (or of a population) is a visualization showing all the possible values (or sometimes referred to as intervals) of the data and how often they occur. When a distribution of categorical data (which we defined earlier in this chapter) is created by a data scientist, it attempts to show the number or percentage of individuals in each group or category.

Linking an earlier defined term with this one, a probability distribution, stated in simple terms, can be thought of as a visualization showing the probability of occurrence of different possible outcomes in an experiment.

Data mining

In Chapter 1, *Transitioning from Data Developer to Data Scientist*, we said, with data mining, one is usually more absorbed in the data relationships (or the potential relationships between points of data, sometimes referred to as variables) and cognitive analysis.

To further define this term, we can mention that data mining is sometimes more simply referred to as knowledge discovery or even just discovery, based upon processing through or analyzing data from new or different viewpoints and summarizing it into valuable insights that can be used to increase revenue, cuts costs, or both.

Using software dedicated to data mining is just one of several analytical approaches to data mining. Although there are tools dedicated to this purpose (such as IBM Cognos BI and Planning Analytics, Tableau, SAS, and so on.), data mining is all about the analysis process finding correlations or patterns among dozens of fields in the data and that can be effectively accomplished using tools such as MS Excel or any number of open source technologies.

 A common technique to data mining is through the creation of custom scripts using tools such as R or Python. In this way, the data scientist has the ability to customize the logic and processing to their exact project needs.

Decision trees

A statistical decision tree uses a diagram that looks like a tree. This structure attempts to represent optional decision paths and a predicted outcome for each path selected. A data scientist will use a decision tree to support, track, and model decision making and their possible consequences, including chance event outcomes, resource costs, and utility. It is a common way to display the logic of a data science process.

Machine learning

Machine learning is one of the most intriguing and exciting areas of data science. It conjures all forms of images around artificial intelligence which includes Neural Networks, **Support Vector Machines (SVMs)**, and so on.

Fundamentally, we can describe the term machine learning as a method of training a computer to make or improve predictions or behaviors based on data or, specifically, relationships within that data. Continuing, machine learning is a process by which predictions are made based upon recognized patterns identified within data, and additionally, it is the ability to continuously learn from the data's patterns, therefore continuingly making better predictions.

It is not uncommon for someone to mistake the process of machine learning for data mining, but data mining focuses more on exploratory data analysis and is known as **unsupervised learning**.

Machine learning can be used to learn and establish baseline behavioral profiles for various entities and then to find meaningful anomalies.

Here is the exciting part: the process of machine learning (using data relationships to make predictions) is known as **predictive analytics**.

Predictive analytics allow the data scientists to produce reliable, repeatable decisions and results and uncover hidden insights through learning from historical relationships and trends in the data.

Munging and wrangling

The terms **munging** and **wrangling** are buzzwords or jargon meant to describe one's efforts to affect the format of data, recordset, or file in some way in an effort to prepare the data for continued or otherwise processing and/or evaluations.

With data development, you are most likely familiar with the idea of **Extract**, **Transform**, and **Load** (**ETL**). In somewhat the same way, a data developer may mung or wrangle data during the transformation steps within an ETL process.

Common munging and wrangling may include removing punctuation or HTML tags, data parsing, filtering, all sorts of transforming, mapping, and tying together systems and interfaces that were not specifically designed to interoperate. Munging can also describe the processing or filtering of raw data into another form, allowing for more convenient consumption of the data elsewhere.

Munging and wrangling might be performed multiple times within a data science process and/or at different steps in the evolving process. Sometimes, data scientists use munging to include various data visualization, data aggregation, training a statistical model, as well as much other potential work. To this point, munging and wrangling may follow a flow beginning with extracting the data in a raw form, performing the munging using various logic, and lastly, placing the resulting content into a structure for use.

Although there are many valid options for munging and wrangling data, preprocessing and manipulation, a tool that is popular with many data scientists today is a product named **Trifecta**, which claims that it is the number one (data) wrangling solution in many industries.

 Trifecta can be downloaded for your personal evaluation from `https://www.trifacta.com/`. Check it out!

Visualization

The main point (although there are other goals and objectives) when leveraging a data visualization technique is to make something complex appear simple. You can think of visualization as any technique for creating a graphic (or similar) to communicate a message.

Other motives for using data visualization include the following:

- To explain the data or put the data in context (which is to highlight demographical statistics)
- To solve a specific problem (for example, identifying problem areas within a particular business model)
- To explore the data to reach a better understanding or add clarity (such as what periods of time do this data span?)
- To highlight or illustrate otherwise invisible data (such as isolating outliers residing in the data)
- To predict, such as potential sales volumes (perhaps based upon seasonality sales statistics)
- And others

Statistical visualization is used in almost every step in the data science process, within the obvious steps such as exploring and visualizing, analyzing and learning, but can also be leveraged during collecting, processing, and the end game of using the identified insights.

D3

D3 or D3.js, is essentially an open source JavaScript library designed with the intention of visualizing data using today's web standards. D3 helps put life into your data, utilizing **Scalable Vector Graphics** (**SVG**), Canvas, and standard HTML.

D3 combines powerful visualization and interaction techniques with a data-driven approach to DOM manipulation, providing data scientists with the full capabilities of modern browsers and the freedom to design the right visual interface that best depicts the objective or assumption.

In contrast to many other libraries, D3.js allows inordinate control over the visualization of data. D3 is embedded within an HTML webpage and uses prebuilt JavaScript functions to select elements, create SVG objects, style them, or add transitions, dynamic effects, and so on.

Regularization

Regularization is one possible approach that a data scientist may use for improving the results generated from a statistical model or data science process, such as when addressing a case of overfitting in statistics and data science.

 We defined fitting earlier in this chapter (fitting describes how well a statistical model or process describes a data scientist's observations). Overfitting is a scenario where a statistical model or process seems to fit too well or appears to be too close to the actual data.

Overfitting usually occurs with an overly simple model. This means that you may have only two variables and are drawing conclusions based on the two. For example, using our previously mentioned example of *daffodil sales*, one might generate a model with temperature as an independent variable and sales as a dependent one. You may see the model fail since it is not as simple as concluding that warmer temperatures will always generate more sales.

In this example, there is a tendency to add more data to the process or model in hopes of achieving a better result. The idea sounds reasonable. For example, you have information such as average rainfall, pollen count, fertilizer sales, and so on; could these data points be added as explanatory variables?

 An explanatory variable is a type of independent variable with a subtle difference. When a variable is independent, it is not affected at all by any other variables. When a variable isn't independent for certain, it's an explanatory variable.

Continuing to add more and more data to your model will have an effect but will probably cause overfitting, resulting in poor predictions since it will closely resemble the data, which is mostly just background noise.

To overcome this situation, a data scientist can use regularization, introducing a tuning parameter (additional factors such as a data points mean value or a minimum or maximum limitation, which gives you the ability to change the complexity or smoothness of your model) into the data science process to solve an ill-posed problem or to prevent overfitting.

Assessment

When a data scientist evaluates a model or data science process for performance, this is referred to as assessment. Performance can be defined in several ways, including the model's growth of learning or the model's ability to improve (with) learning (to obtain a better score) with additional experience (for example, more rounds of training with additional samples of data) or accuracy of its results.

One popular method of assessing a model or processes performance is called **bootstrap sampling**. This method examines performance on certain subsets of data, repeatedly generating results that can be used to calculate an estimate of accuracy (performance).

The bootstrap sampling method takes a random sample of data, splits it into three files--a training file, a testing file, and a validation file. The model or process logic is developed based on the data in the training file and then evaluated (or tested) using the testing file. This tune and then test process is repeated until the data scientist is comfortable with the results of the tests. At that point, the model or process is again tested, this time using the validation file, and the results should provide a true indication of how it will perform.

You can imagine using the bootstrap `sampling` method to develop program logic by analyzing test data to determine logic flows and then running (or testing) your logic against the test data file. Once you are satisfied that your logic handles all of the conditions and exceptions found in your testing data, you can run a final test on a new, never-before-seen data file for a final validation test.

Cross-validation

Cross-validation is a method for assessing a data science process performance. Mainly used with predictive modeling to estimate how accurately a model might perform in practice, one might see cross-validation used to check how a model will potentially generalize, in other words, how the model can apply what it infers from samples to an entire population (or recordset).

With cross-validation, you identify a (known) dataset as your validation dataset on which training is run along with a dataset of unknown data (or first seen data) against which the model will be tested (this is known as your **testing dataset**). The objective is to ensure that problems such as overfitting (allowing non-inclusive information to influence results) are controlled and also provide an insight into how the model will generalize a real problem or on a real data file.

The cross-validation process will consist of separating data into samples of similar subsets, performing the analysis on one subset (called the **training set**) and validating the analysis on the other subset (called the **validation set** or **testing set**). To reduce variability, multiple iterations (also called **folds** or **rounds**) of cross-validation are performed using different partitions, and the validation results are averaged over the rounds. Typically, a data scientist will use a models stability to determine the actual number of rounds of cross-validation that should be performed.

Neural networks

Neural networks are also called **artificial neural networks** (**ANNs**), and the objective is to solve problems in the same way that the human brain would.

Google will provide the following explanation of ANN as stated in *Neural Network Primer: Part I, by Maureen Caudill, AI Expert, Feb. 1989*:

> *A computing system made up of several simple, highly interconnected processing elements, which process information by their dynamic state response to external inputs.*

To oversimplify the idea of neural networks, recall the concept of software encapsulation, and consider a computer program with an input layer, a processing layer, and an output layer. With this thought in mind, understand that neural networks are also organized in a network of these layers, usually with more than a single processing layer.

Patterns are presented to the network by way of the input layer, which then communicates to one (or more) of the processing layers (where the actual processing is done). The processing layers then link to an output layer where the result is presented.

Most neural networks will also contain some form of learning rule that modifies the weights of the connections (in other words, the network learns which processing nodes perform better and gives them a heavier weight) per the input patterns that it is presented with. In this way (in a sense), neural networks learn by example as a child learns to recognize a cat from being exposed to examples of cats.

Boosting

In a manner of speaking, boosting is a process generally accepted in data science for improving the accuracy of a weak learning data science process.

 Data science processes defined as weak learners are those that produce results that are only slightly better than if you would randomly guess the outcome. Weak learners are basically thresholds or a 1-level decision tree.

Specifically, boosting is aimed at reducing bias and variance in supervised learning.

What do we mean by bias and variance? Before going on further about boosting, let's take note of what we mean by bias and variance.

Data scientists describe bias as a level of favoritism that is present in the data collection process, resulting in uneven, disingenuous results and can occur in a variety of different ways. A `sampling` method is called **biased** if it systematically favors some outcomes over others.

A variance may be defined (by a data scientist) simply as the distance from a variable mean (or how far from the average a result is).

The boosting method can be described as a data scientist repeatedly running through a data science process (that has been identified as a weak learning process), with each iteration running on different and random examples of data sampled from the original population recordset. All the results (or classifiers or residue) produced by each run are then combined into a single merged result (that is a gradient).

This concept of using a random subset of the original recordset for each iteration originates from bootstrap sampling in bagging and has a similar variance-reducing effect on the combined model.

In addition, some data scientists consider boosting a means to convert weak learners into strong ones; in fact, to some, the process of boosting simply means turning a weak learner into a strong learner.

Lift

In data science, the term lift compares the frequency of an observed pattern within a recordset or population with how frequently you might expect to see that same pattern occur within the data by chance or randomly.

If the lift is very low, then typically, a data scientist will expect that there is a very good probability that the pattern identified is occurring just by chance. The larger the lift, the more likely it is that the pattern is real.

Mode

In statistics and data science, when a data scientist uses the term mode, he or she refers to the value that occurs most often within a sample of data. Mode is not calculated but is determined manually or through processing of the data.

Outlier

Outliers can be defined as follows:

- A data point that is way out of keeping with the others
- That piece of data that doesn't fit
- Either a very high value or a very low value
- Unusual observations within the data
- An observation point that is distant from all others

Predictive modeling

The development of statistical models and/or data science processes to predict future events is called **predictive modeling**.

Big Data

Again, we have some variation of the definition of big data. A large assemblage of data, data sets that are so large or complex that traditional data processing applications are inadequate, and data about every aspect of our lives have all been used to define or refer to big data. In 2001, then Gartner analyst Doug Laney introduced the 3V's concept.

You can refer to the link:
http://blogs.gartner.com/doug-laney/files/2012/01/ad949-3D-Data-
Management-Controlling-Data-Volume-Velocity-and-
Variety.pdf</span>

The 3V's, as per Laney, are volume, variety, and velocity. The V's make up the dimensionality of big data: volume (or the measurable amount of data), variety (meaning the number of types of data), and velocity (referring to the speed of processing or dealing with that data).

Confidence interval

The confidence interval is a range of values that a data scientist will specify around an estimate to indicate their margin of error, combined with a probability that a value will fall in that range. In other words, confidence intervals are good estimates of the unknown population parameter.

Writing

Although visualizations grab much more of the limelight when it comes to presenting the output or results of a data science process or predictive model, writing skills are still not only an important part of how a data scientist communicates but still considered an essential skill for all data scientists to be successful.

Summary

In this chapter, we said that, currently, how data science is defined is a matter of opinion. A practical explanation is that data science is a progression or, even better, an evolution of thought, consisting of collecting, processing, exploring, and visualizing data, analyzing (data) and/or applying machine learning (to the data), and then deciding (or planning) based upon acquired insight(s).

Then, with the goal of thinking like a data scientist, we introduced and defined a number of common terms and concepts a data scientist should be comfortable with.

In the next chapter, we will present and explain how a data developer might understand and approach the topic of data cleaning using several common statistical methods.

3
A Developer's Approach to Data Cleaning

This chapter discusses how a developer might understand and approach the topic of **data cleaning** using several common statistical methods.

In this chapter, we've broken things into the following topics:

- Understanding basic data cleaning
- Using R to detect and diagnose common data issues, such as missing values, special values, outliers, inconsistencies, and localization
- Using R to address advanced statistical situations, such as transformation, deductive correction, and deterministic imputation

Understanding basic data cleaning

The importance of having clean (and therefore reliable) data in any statistical project cannot be overstated. Dirty data, even with sound statistical practice, can be unreliable and can lead to producing results that suggest courses of action that are incorrect or that may even cause harm or financial loss. It has been stated that a data scientist spends nearly 90 percent of his or her time in the process of cleaning data and only 10 percent on the actual modeling of the data and deriving results from it.

So, just what is data cleaning?

Data cleaning is also referred to as data cleansing or data scrubbing and involves both the processes of detecting as well as addressing errors, omissions, and inconsistencies within a population of data.

This may be done interactively with data wrangling tools, or in batch mode through scripting. We will use R in this book as it is well-fitted for data science since it works with even very complex datasets, allows handling of the data through various modeling functions, and even provides the ability to generate visualizations to represent data and prove theories and assumptions in just a few lines of code.

During cleansing, you first use logic to examine and evaluate your data pool to establish a level of quality for the data. The level of data quality can be affected by the way the data is entered, stored, and managed. Cleansing can involve correcting, replacing, or just removing data points or entire actual records.

Cleansing should not be confused with validating as they differ from each other. A validation process is a pass or fails process, usually occurring as the data is captured (time of entry), rather than an operation performed later on the data in preparation for an intended purpose.

As a data developer, one should not be new to the concept of data cleaning or the importance of improving the level of quality of data. A data developer will also agree that the process of addressing data quality requires a routine and regular review and evaluation of the data, and in fact, most organizations have enterprise tools and/or processes (or at least policies) in place to routinely preprocess and cleanse the enterprise data.

There is quite a list of both free and paid tools to sample, if you are interested, including iManageData, Data Manager, DataPreparator (Trifecta) Wrangler, and so on. From a statistical perspective, the top choices would be R, Python, and Julia.

Before you can address specific issues within your data, you need to detect them. Detecting them requires that you determine what would qualify as an issue or error, given the context of your objective (more on this later in this section).

Common data issues

We can categorize data difficulties into several groups. The most generally accepted groupings (of data issues) include:

- **Accuracy**: There are many varieties of data inaccuracies and the most common examples include poor math, out-of-range values, invalid values, duplication, and more.

- **Completeness**: Data sources may be missing values from particular columns, missing entire columns, or even missing complete transactions.

- **Update status**: As part of your quality assurance, you need to establish the cadence of data refresh or update, as well as have the ability to determine when the data was last saved or updated. This is also referred to as latency.

- **Relevance**: It is identification and elimination of information that you don't need or care about, given your objectives. An example would be removing sales transactions for pickles if you are intending on studying personal grooming products.

- **Consistency**: It is common to have to cross-reference or translate information from data sources. For example, recorded responses to a patient survey may require translation to a single consistent indicator to later make processing or visualizing easier.

- **Reliability**: This is chiefly concerned with making sure that the method of data gathering leads to consistent results. A common data assurance process involves establishing baselines and ranges, and then routinely verifying that the data results fall within the established expectations. For example, districts that typically have a mix of both registered Democrat and Republican voters would warrant the investigation if the data suddenly was 100 percent single partied.

- **Appropriateness**: Data is considered appropriate if it is suitable for the intended purpose; this can be subjective. For example, it is considered a fact that holiday traffic affects purchasing habits (an increase in US Flags Memorial day week does not indicate an average or expected weekly behavior).

- **Accessibility**: Data of interest may be watered down in a sea of data you are not interested in, thereby reducing the quality of the interesting data since it would be mostly inaccessible. This is particularly common in big data projects. Additionally, security may play a role in the quality of your data. For example, particular computers might be excluded from captured logging files or certain health-related information may be hidden and not part of shared patient data.

Contextual data issues

A lot of the previously mentioned data issues can be automatically detected and even corrected. The issues may have been originally caused by user entry errors, by corruption in transmission or storage, or by different definitions or understandings of similar entities in different data sources. In data science, there is more to think about.

During data cleaning, a data scientist will attempt to identify patterns within the data, based on a hypothesis or assumption about the context of the data and its intended purpose. In other words, any data that the data scientist determines to be either obviously disconnected with the assumption or objective of the data or obviously inaccurate will then be addressed. This process is reliant upon the data scientist's judgment and his or her ability to determine which points are valid and which are not.

 When relying on human judgment, there is always a chance that valid data points, not sufficiently accounted for in the data scientist's hypothesis/assumption, are overlooked or incorrectly addressed. Therefore, it is a common practice to maintain appropriately labeled versions of your cleansed data.

Cleaning techniques

Typically, the data cleansing process evolves around identifying those data points that are outliers, or those data points that stand out for not following the pattern within the data that the data scientist sees or is interested in.

The data scientists use various methods or techniques for identifying the outliers in the data. One approach is plotting the data points and then visually inspecting the resultant plot for those data points that lie far outside the general distribution. Another technique is programmatically eliminating all points that do not meet the data scientist's mathematical control limits (limits based upon the objective or intention of the statistical project).

Other data cleaning techniques include:

- **Validity checking**: Validity checking involves applying rules to the data to determine if it is valid or not. These rules can be global; for example, a data scientist could perform a uniqueness check if specific unique keys are part of the data pool (for example, social security numbers cannot be duplicated), or case level, as when a combination of field values must be a certain value. The validation may be strict (such as removing records with missing values) or fuzzy (such as correcting values that partially match existing, known values).
- **Enhancement**: This is a technique where data is made complete by adding related information. The additional information can be calculated by using the existing values within the data file or it can be added from another source. This information could be used for reference, comparison, contrast, or show tendencies.

- **Harmonization**: With data harmonization, data values are converted, or mapped to other more desirable values.
- **Standardization**: This involves changing a reference dataset to a new standard. For example, use of standard codes.
- **Domain expertise**: This involves removing or modifying data values in a data file based upon the data scientist's prior experience or best judgment.

We will go through an example of each of these techniques in the next sections of this chapter.

R and common data issues

Let's start this section with some background on R. R is a language and environment that is easy to learn, very flexible in nature, and very focused on statistical computing, making it a great choice for manipulating, cleaning, summarizing, producing probability statistics, and so on.

In addition, here are a few more reasons to use R for data cleaning:

- It is used by a large number of data scientists so it's not going away anytime soon
- R is platform independent, so what you create will run almost anywhere
- R has awesome help resources--just Google it, you'll see!

Outliers

The simplest explanation for what outliers are might be is to say that outliers are those data points that just don't fit the rest of your data. Upon observance, any data that is either very high, very low, or just unusual (within the context of your project), is an outlier. As part of data cleansing, a data scientist would typically identify the outliers and then address the outliers using a generally accepted method:

- Delete the outlier values or even the actual variable where the outliers exist
- Transform the values or the variable itself

Let's look at a real-world example of using R to identify and then address data outliers.

In the world of gaming, slot machines (a gambling machine operated by inserting coins into a slot and pulling a handle which determines the payoff) are quite popular. Most slot machines today are electronic and therefore are programmed in such a way that all their activities are continuously tracked. In our example, investors in a casino want to use this data (as well as various supplementary data) to drive adjustments to their profitability strategy. In other words, what makes for a profitable slot machine? Is it the machine's theme or its type? Are newer machines more profitable than older or retro machines? What about the physical location of the machine? Are lower denomination machines more profitable? We try to find our answers using the outliers.

We are given a collection or pool of gaming data (formatted as a comma-delimited or CSV text file), which includes data points such as the location of the slot machine, its denomination, month, day, year, machine type, age of the machine, promotions, coupons, weather, and coin-in (which is the total amount inserted into the machine less pay-outs). The first step for us as a data scientist is to review (sometimes called **profile**) the data, where we'll determine if any outliers exist. The second step will be to address those outliers.

Step 1 – Profiling the data

R makes this step very simple. Although there are many ways to program a solution, let us try to keep the lines of the actual program code or script to a minimum. We can begin by defining our CSV file as a variable in our R session (named `MyFile`) and then reading our file into an R `data.frame` (named `MyData`):

```
MyFile <-"C:/GammingData/SlotsResults.csv"
MyData <- read.csv(file=MyFile, header=TRUE, sep=",")
```

In statistics, a `boxplot` is a simple way to gain information regarding the shape, variability, and centre (or median) of a statistical dataset, so we'll use the `boxplot` with our data to see if we can identify both the median `Coin-in` and if there are any outliers. To do this, we can ask R to plot the `Coin-in` value for each slot machine in our file, using the `boxplot` function:

```
boxplot(MyData[11],main='Gamming Data Review', ylab = "Coin-in")
```

 `Coin-in` is the 11th column in our file so I am referring to it explicitly as a parameter of the function `boxplot`. I've also added optional parameters (again, continuing the effort to stay minimal) which add headings to the visualization.

Executing the previous script yields us the following visual. Note both the median (shown by the line that cuts through the box in the `boxplot`) as well as the four outliers:

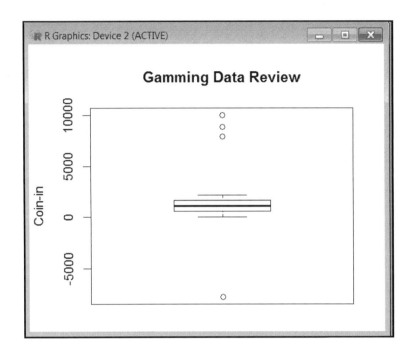

Step 2 – Addressing the outliers

Now that we see the outliers do exist within our data, we can address them so that they do not adversely affect our intended study. Firstly, we know that it is illogical to have a negative `Coin-in` value since machines cannot dispense more coins that have been inserted in them. Given this rule, we can simply drop any records from the file that have negative `Coin-in` values. Again, R makes it easy as we'll use the `subset` function to create a new version of our `data.frame`, one that only has records (or cases) with non-negative `Coin-in` values.

We'll call our `subset` data frame noNegs:

```
noNegs <- subset(MyData, MyData[11]>0)
```

Then, we'll replot to make sure we've dropped our negative outlier:

```
boxplot(noNegs[11],main='Gamming Data Review', ylab = "Coin-in")
```

This produces a new `boxplot`, as shown in the following screenshot:

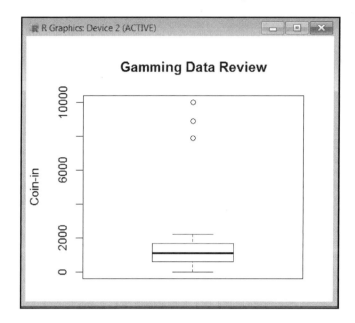

We can use the same approach to drop our extreme positive `Coin-in` values (those greater than $1,500) by creating yet another `subset` and then replotting:

```
noOutliers <-subset(noNegs, noNegs[11]<1500)
boxplot(noOutliers[11],main='Gamming Data Review', ylab = "Coin-in")
```

It is well-advised, as you work through various iterations of your data, that you save off most (if not just the most significant) versions of your data. You can use the R function `write.csv`:

```
write.csv(noOutliers, file = "C:/GammingData/MyData_lessOutliers.csv")
```

 Most data scientists adopt a common naming convention to be used through the project (if not for all the projects). The names of your files should be as explicit as possible to save you time later. In addition, especially when working with big data, you need to be mindful of disk space.

The output of the preceding code is as follows:

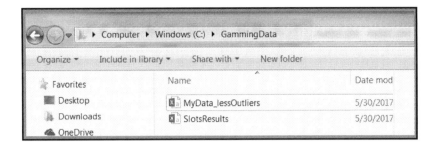

Domain expertise

Moving on, another data cleaning technique is referred to as cleaning data based upon domain expertise. This doesn't need to be complicated. The point of this technique is simply using information not found in the data. For example, previously we excluded cases with negative `Coin-in` values since we know it is impossible to have a negative `Coin-in` amount. Another example might be the time when Hurricane Sandy hit the northeast United States. During that period of time, the cases of most machines had very low (if not zero) `Coin-in` amounts. A data scientist would probably remove all the data cases during a specific time period, based on that information.

Validity checking

As I mentioned earlier in this chapter, cross-validation is when a data scientist applies rules to data in a data pool.

 Validity checking is the most common form of statistical data cleansing and is a process that both the data developer and the data scientist will most likely be (at least somewhat) familiar with.

There can be any number of validity rules used to clean the data, and these rules will depend upon the intended purpose or objective of the data scientist. Examples of these rules include: data-typing (for example, a field must be a numeric), range limitations (where numbers or dates must fall within a certain range), required (a value cannot be empty or missing), uniqueness (a field, or a combination of fields, must be unique within the data pool), set-member (this is when values must be a member of a discreet list), foreign-key (certain values found within a case must be defined as member of or meeting a particular rule), regular expression patterning (which simply means verifying that a value is formatted in a prescribed format), and cross-field validation (where combinations of fields within a case must meet a certain criteria).

Let's look at a few examples of the preceding, starting with data-typing (also known as **coercion**). R offers six coercion functions to make it easy:

- `as.numeric`
- `as.integer`
- `as.character`
- `as.logical`
- `as.factor`
- `as.ordered`
- `as.Date`

These functions, along with a little R knowledge, can make the effort of converting a value in a data pool pretty straightforward. For example, using the previous GammingData as an example, we might discover that a new gamming results file was generated and the age value was saved as a string (or text value). To clean it, we need to convert the value to a numeric data type. We can use the following single line of R code to quickly convert those values in the file:

```
noOutliers["Age"]<-as.numeric(noOutliers["Age"])
```

One point: using this simple approach, should any value be unable to be converted, it will be set to an **NA** value. In type conversion, the real work is understanding what type a value needs to be, and, of course, what data types are valid; R has a wide variety of data types, including scalars, vectors (numerical, character, logical), matrices, data frames, and lists.

Another area of data cleaning we'll look at here is the process of regular expression patterning. In practice, especially when working with data that is collected (or mined) from multiple sources, the data scientist surely encounters either field that are not in the desired format (for the objective at hand) or, field values that are inconsistently formatted (which potentially can yield incorrect results). Some examples can be dates, social security numbers, and telephone numbers. With dates, depending on the source, you may have to re-type (as described previously), but more often than not, you'll also need to reformat the values into a format that is usable, given your objective.

Re-typing a date is important so that R knows to use the value as an actual date and you can use the various R data functions correctly.

A common example is when data contains cases with dates that are perhaps formatted as YYYY/MM/DD and you want to perform a time series analysis showing a sum week to week, or some other operation that requires using the date value but perhaps requiring the date to be reformatted, or you just need it to be a true R date object type. So, let's assume a new Gamming file—this one with just two columns of data: Date and Coinin. This file is a dump of collected Coinin values for a single slot machine, day by day.

The records (or cases) in our new file look like the following screenshot:

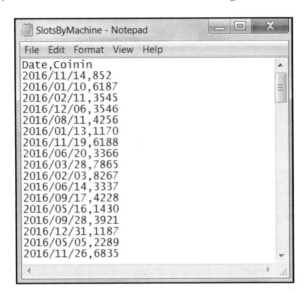

A variety of cleaning examples can be used by the data scientist. Starting with verifying what data types each of these data points are. We can use the R function class to verify our file's data types. First (as we did in the previous example), we read our CSV file into an R data frame object:

```
MyFile <-"C:/GammingData/SlotsByMachine.csv"
MyData <- read.csv(file=MyFile, header=TRUE, sep=",")
```

Next, we can use the `class` function, as shown in the following screenshot:

```
R RGui (64-bit) - [R Console]

R File  Edit  View  Misc  Packages  Windows  Help

> MyFile <-"C:/GammingData/SlotsByMachine.csv"
> MyData <- read.csv(file=MyFile, header=TRUE, se
> class(MyData)
[1] "data.frame"
> class(MyData$Date)
[1] "factor"
> class(MyData$Coinin)
[1] "integer"
> |
```

You can see in the preceding screenshot that we used `class` to display our data types.

`MyData` is our data frame holding our gaming data, `Date` is of type `factor`, and `Coinin` is an `integer`. So, the data frame and the integer should make sense to you, but take note that R sets our dates up for what it calls a `factor`. Factors are categorical variables that are beneficial in summary statistics, plots, and regressions, but not so much as date values. To remedy this, we can use the R functions `substr` and `paste` as shown next:

```
MyData$Date<-paste(substr(MyData$Date,6,7), substr(MyData$Date,9,10),
substr(MyData$Date,1,4),sep="/")
```

This reformats the value of our `Data` field in all our cases in one simple line of script by pulling apart the field into three segments (the month, day, and year) and then pasting the segments back together in the order we want (with a/as the separator (`sep`)), as shown in the following screenshot:

```
> MyFile <-"C:/GammingData/SlotsByMachine.csv"
> MyData <- read.csv(file=MyFile, header=TRUE, sep=",")
> MyData$Date<-paste(substr(MyData$Date,6,7),substr(MyData$Date,9,10),substr(MyData$Date,1,4),sep="/")
> class(MyData$Date)
[1] "character"
>
```

We find that this line of script converts our `Data` field to type `character` and, finally, we can use them `as.Date` function to re-data type our values to an R `Date` type:

```
> MyFile <-"C:/GammingData/SlotsByMachine.csv"
> MyData <- read.csv(file=MyFile, header=TRUE, sep=",")
> MyData$Date<-paste(substr(MyData$Date,6,7),substr(MyData$Date,9,10),substr(MyData$Date,1,4),sep="/")
> class(MyData$Date)
[1] "character"
> MyData$Date<-as.Date(MyData$Date, format="%m/%d/%Y")
> class(MyData$Date)
[1] "Date"
>
```

With a little trial and error, you can reformat a string or character data point exactly how you want it.

Enhancing data

Data cleaning through enhancement is another common technique where data is made complete (and perhaps more valuable) by adding related information, facts, and/or figures. The source of this additional data could be calculations using information already in the data or added from another source. There are a variety of reasons why a data scientist may take the time to enhance data.

Based upon the purpose or objective at hand, the information the data scientist adds might be used for reference, comparison, contrast, or show tendencies. Typical use cases include:

- Derived fact calculation
- Indicating the use of calendar versus fiscal year
- Converting time zones

- Currency conversions
- Adding current versus previous period indicators
- Calculating values such as the total units shipped per day
- Maintaining slowly changing dimensions

 As a data scientist, you should always use scripting to enhance your data, as this approach is much better than editing a data file directly since it is less prone to errors and maintains the integrity of the original file. Also, creating scripts allows you to reapply the enhancements to multiple files and/or new versions of files received, without having to redo the same work.

For a working example, let us again go back to our GammingData. Assume we're receiving files of the Coinin amounts by slot machine and our gaming company now runs casinos outside of the continental United States. These locations are sending us files to be included in our statistical analysis and we've now discovered that these international files are providing the Coinin amounts in their local currencies. To be able to correctly model the data, we'll need to convert those amounts to US dollars. Here is the scenario:

File Source: Great Britain

Currency used: GBP or Great British Pound

The formula to convert our GBP values to USD is simply the amount multiplied by an exchange rate. So, in R:

```
MyData$Coinin<-MyData$Coinin * 1.4
```

The previous line of code will accomplish what we want; however, the data scientist is left to determine which currency needs to be converted (GBP) and what the exchange rate to be used is. Not a huge deal, but one might want to experiment with creating a user-defined function that determines the rate to be used, as shown next:

```
getRate <- function(arg){
    if(arg=="GPB") {
      myRate <- 1.4
    }
    if(arg=="CAD") {
      myRate <- 1.34
    }
    return(myRate)
}
```

Although the preceding code snippet is rather simplistic, it illustrates the point of creating logic that we can reuse later:

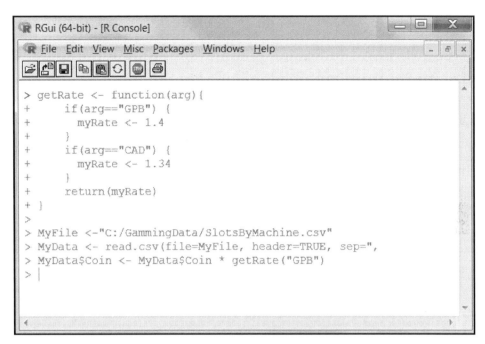

Finally, to make things better still, save off your function (in an R file) so that it can always be used:

```
source("C:/GammingData/CurerncyLogic.R")
```

Then:

```
MyFile <-"C:/GammingData/SlotsByMachine.csv"
MyData <- read.csv(file=MyFile, header=TRUE, sep=",")
MyData$Coin <- MyData$Coinin * getRate("CAD")
```

 Of course, in the best of all worlds, we might modify the function to look up the rate in a table or a file, based upon the country code, so that the rates can be changed to reflect the most current value and to de-couple the data from the program code.

Harmonization

With data harmonization, the data scientist converts, translates, or maps data values to other more desirable values, based upon the overall objective or purpose of the analysis to be performed. The most common examples of this can be gender or country code. For example, if your file has gender coded as 1s and 0s or M and F, you might want to convert the data points to be consistently coded as MALE or FEMALE.

With country codes, the data scientist may want to plot summations for regions: North America, South America, and Europe rather than USA, CA, MX, BR, CH, GB, FR, and DE individually. In this case, he or she would be creating aggregated values:

North America = USA + CA + MX

South America = BR + CH

Europe = GB + FR + DE

To make a point, perhaps the data scientist has stitched together multiple survey files, all containing gender, called gender.txt, but in various codes (1, 0, M, F, Male, and Female). If we tried to use the R function table, we would see the following undesirable result:

```
R RGui (64-bit) - [R Console]
R File  Edit  View  Misc  Packages  Windows  Help

> MyFile <-"C:/GammingData/Gender.txt"
> MyData <- read.csv(file=MyFile, header=TRUE, sep=",")
> table(MyData)
MyData
      0       1       F  Female       M    Male
    382     359     339     347     358     346
> |
```

And if we visualize this with the best of expectations:

```
lbs = c("Male", "Female")
pie(table(MyData), main="Gambling by Gender")
```

We see the following screenshot:

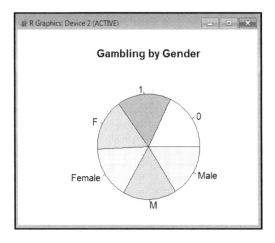

Once again, to solve the inconsistent coding of the data point gender, I've borrowed the concept from the example in the previous section and created a simple function to help us with our recoding:

```
setGender <- function(arg){
    if(substr(arg,1,1)=="0" | toupper(substr(arg,1,1))=="M") { Gender <-
"MALE" }
    if(substr(arg,1,1)=="1" | toupper(substr(arg,1,1))=="F") { Gender <-
"FEMALE" }
    return(Gender)
}
```

This time, I've added the `toupper` function so that we don't have to worry about the case, as well as `substr` to handle values that are longer than a single character.

 I am assuming the argument value will be either 0,1,m,M,f,F,Male, or Female, otherwise an error will occur.

Since R categorizes the `Gender` value as data type `factor`, I found it was difficult to easily make use of the simple function, so I decided to create a new R data frame object to hold our harmonized data. I've also decided to use a looping process to read through each case (record) in our file and convert it to `Male` or `Female`:

```
MyFile <-"C:/GammingData/Gender.txt"
MyData <- read.csv(file=MyFile, header=TRUE, sep=",")
GenderData <-data.frame(nrow(MyData))
for(i in 2:nrow(MyData))
{
    x<-as.character(MyData[i,1])
    GenderData[i,1] <-setGender(x)
}
```

Now we can enjoy a more appropriate visualization by writing:

```
lbls = c("Male", "Female")
pie(table(GenderData), labels=lbls, main="Gambling by Gender")
```

The output of the preceding code is as follows:

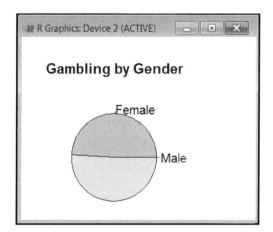

Standardization

Most mainstream data scientists have noted the importance of standardizing data variables (changing reference data to a standard) as part of the data cleaning process before beginning a statistical study or analysis project. This is important, as, without standardization, the data points measured using different scales will most likely not contribute equally to the analysis.

If you consider that a data point within a range between 0 and 100 will outweigh a variable within a range between 0 and 1, you can understand the importance of data standardization. Using these variables without standardization in effect gives the variable with the larger range a larger weight in the analysis. To address this concern and equalize the variables, the data scientists try to transform the data into a comparable scale.

Centring (of the data points) is the most common example of data standardization (there are many others though). To center a data point, the data scientist would subtract the mean of all the data points from each individual data point in the file.

Instead of doing the mathematics, R provides the `scale` function. This is a function whose default method centers and/or scales a column of numeric data in a file in one line of code. Let's look at a simple example.

Back to our slot machines! In our gaming files, you may recall that there is a field named `Coinin` that contains a numeric value indicating the total dollars put into the machine. This is considered a measurement of the machine profitability. This seems like an obvious data point to use in our profitability analysis. However, these amounts may be misleading since there are machines of different denominations (in other words, some machines accept nickels while others accept dimes or dollars). Perhaps this difference in machine denominations creates an unequal scale. We can use the `scale` function to address this situation. First, we see in the following screenshot, the values of `Coin.in`:

```
R Console

> MyFile <-"C:/GammingData/SlotsResults.csv"
> MyData <- read.csv(file=MyFile, header=TRUE, sep=",")
> MyData[11]
       Coin.in
1         9999
2         1505
3          673
4          872
5         7900
6          671
7          475
8         1750
9         8888
10          88
11         790
12       -7792
13        1030
14         353
15         823
16        1789
17        1648
```

We can then write the following line of code to center our `Coin.in` data points:

```
scale(MyData[11], center = TRUE, scale = TRUE)
```

The value of center determines how column centring is to be performed. Using center is TRUE causes centring to be done by subtracting the column means (omitting NAs) of `Coin.in` from their corresponding columns. The value of `scale` determines how column scaling is performed (after centring). If the scale is TRUE, then scaling is done by dividing the (centered) columns of `Coin.in` by their standard deviations if a center is TRUE, and the root mean square otherwise.

We see the difference in the following screenshot:

```
R Console

> MyFile <-"C:/GammingData/SlotsResults.csv"
> MyData <- read.csv(file=MyFile, header=TRUE, sep=",")
> scale(MyData[11], center = TRUE, scale = TRUE)
               Coin.in
 [1,]   1.200796e+01
 [2,]   5.190288e-01
 [3,]  -6.063296e-01
 [4,]  -3.371633e-01
 [5,]   9.168869e+00
 [6,]  -6.090348e-01
 [7,]  -8.741432e-01
 [8,]   8.504144e-01
 [9,]   1.050523e+01
[10,]  -1.397597e+00
[11,]  -4.480760e-01
[12,]  -1.205604e+01
[13,]  -1.234534e-01
[14,]  -1.039160e+00
[15,]  -4.034404e-01
[16,]   9.031655e-01
[17,]   7.124498e-01
```

Transformations

A thought-provoking type of data cleaning, which may be a new concept for a data developer, is **data transformation**. Data transformation is a process where the data scientist actually changes what you might expect to be valid data values through some mathematical operation.

Performing data transformation maps data from an original format into the format expected by an appropriate application or a format more convenient for a particular assumption or purpose. This includes value conversions or translation functions, as well as normalizing of numeric values to conform to the minimum and maximum values.

As we've used R earlier in this chapter, we can see that the syntax of a very simple example of this process is simple. For example, a data scientist may decide to transform a given value to the square root of the value:

```
data.dat$trans_Y <-sqrt(data.dat$Y)
```

The preceding code example informs R to create a new variable (or column in the `data.dat` dataset) named `trans_Y` that is equal to the square root of the original response variable `Y`.

 While R can support just about any mathematical operation you can think of or have a need for, the syntax is not always intuitive. R even provides the generic function `transform`, but as of this writing, it only works with data frames. `transform.default` converts its first argument to a data frame and then calls `transform.data.frame`.

But why would you do this? Well, one reason is relationships like that wouldn't work well. For example, if you were experimenting with values that were different by orders of magnitude, it would be difficult to deal or work with them. Practical examples can be a comparison of the physical body weight between species or various sound frequencies and their effects on the atmosphere. In these examples, the use of log transformations enables the data scientist to graph values in a way that permits one to see the differences among the data points at lower values.

Another example is the transformation of test scores (to the distance the score is from a mean score).

Finally, various widely used statistical methods assume normality or a normal distribution shape. In cases where the data scientist observes something other than normalcy, data transformations can be used. Data transformations such as log or exponential, or power transformations are typically used in an attempt to make the distribution of data scores that are non-normal in shape more normal. These data transformations can also help the data scientist bring extreme outliers closer to the rest of the data values; and that reduces the impact of the outliers on the estimates of summary statistics, such as the sample mean or correlation.

Deductive correction

With deductive reasoning, one uses known information, assumptions, or generally accepted rules to reach a conclusion. In statistics, a data scientist uses this concept (in an attempt) to repair inconsistencies and/or missing values within a data population.

To the data developer, examples of deductive correction include the idea of converting a string or text value to a numeric data type or flipping a sign from negative to positive (or vice versa). Practical examples of these instances are overcoming storage limitations such as when survey information is always captured and stored as text or when accounting needs to represent a numeric dollar value as an expense. In these cases, a review of the data may take place (in order to deduce what corrections—also known as **statistical dataediting**—need to be performed), or the process may be automated to affect all incoming data from a particular data source.

Other deductive corrections routinely performed by the data scientists include the corrections of input typing errors, rounding errors, sign errors, and value interchanges.

There are R packages and libraries available, such as the `deducorrect` package, which focus on the correction of rounding, typing, and sign errors, and include three data cleaning algorithms (`correctRounding`, `correctTypos`, and `correctSigns`). However, the data scientists mostly want to specially custom script a solution for the project at hand.

Deterministic imputation

We have been discussing the topic of the data scientists deducing or determining how to address or correct a dirty data issue, such as missing, incorrect, incomplete, or inconsistent values within a data pool.

When data is missing (or incorrect, incomplete, or inconsistent) within a data pool, it can make handling and analysis difficult and can introduce bias to the results of the analysis performed on the data. This leads us to imputation.

In data statistics, imputation is when, through a data cleansing procedure, the data scientist replaces missing (or otherwise specified) data with other values.

Because missing data can create problems in analyzing data, imputation is seen as a way to avoid the dangers involved with simply discarding or removing altogether the cases with missing values. In fact, some statistical packages default to discarding any case that has a missing value, which may introduce bias or affect the representativeness of the results. Imputation preserves all the cases within the data pool by replacing the missing data with an estimated value based on other available information.

Deterministic imputation is a process used by the data scientists in the process of assigning replacement values for missing, invalid, or inconsistent data that has failed edits. In other words, in a particular case, when specific values of all other fields are known and valid, if only one (missing) value will cause the record or case to satisfy or pass all the data scientist edits, that value will be imputed. Deterministic imputation is a conservation imputation theory in that it is aimed at cases that are simply identified (as mentioned previously) and may be the first situation that is considered in the automated editing and imputation of data.

Currently, in the field of data science, imputation theory is gaining popularity and is continuing to be developed, and thus requires consistent attention to new information regarding the subject.

A few of the other well-known imputation theories attempting to deal with missing data include hot deck and cold deck imputation; listwise and pairwise deletion; mean imputation; regression imputation; last observation carried forward; stochastic imputation; and multiple imputations.

Summary

In this chapter, we provided an overview of the fundamentals of the different kinds or types of statistical data cleansing. Then, using the R programming language, we illustrated various working examples, showing each of the best or commonly used data cleansing techniques.

We also introduced the concepts of data transformation, deductive correction, and deterministic imputation.

In the next chapter, we will dive deep into the topic of what data mining is and why it is important, and use R for the most common statistical data mining methods: dimensional reduction, frequent patterns, and sequences.

4

Data Mining and the Database Developer

This chapter introduces the data developer to mining (not to be confused with querying) data, providing an understanding of exactly what data mining is and why it is an integral part of data science.

We'll provide working examples to help the reader feel comfortable using R for the most common statistical data mining methods: dimensional reduction, frequent patterns, and sequences.

In this chapter, we've broken things into the following topics:

- Definition and purpose of data mining
- Preparing the developer for data mining rather than data querying
- Using R for dimensional reduction, frequent patterns, and sequence mining

Data mining

It is always prudent to start explaining things with a high-level definition.

Data mining can be explained simply as assembling information concerning a particular topic or belief in an understandable (and further useable) format. Keep in mind though that the information assembled is not the data itself (as with data querying) but information from the data (more on this later in this chapter).

Data mining should also not be confused with analytics, information extraction, or data analysis. Also, it can be manual or by hand, a semi-automatic, or automatic process. When working with new data, it will typically be a manual process that the data scientist will perform. Later, when working with newer versions of the same data (source), it may become automated to some level or degree.

Data mining is the probing carried out by a data scientist to find previously unknown information within the data, such as:

- Patterns, such as groups of data records, known as **clusters**
- Unusual records, known as **anomalies**
- Dependencies in the form of association rules or sequential patterns

This new information (or insights) can be thought of as a kind of data summary and can be used in further analysis or, for example, in machine learning and predictive analytics. For example, with data mining, a data scientist might identify various groups that can then be used to obtain more accurate prediction results by a decision support system.

 Data developers can liken the insights derived from data mining to descriptive or structural metadata, which is understood within the industry as data that defines data.

Once the probing is completed and the data scientist has mined the information, that information must then be transformed into a comprehensible and usable structure, given the objectives of the effort.

 Data collection, data preparation, results from interpretation and visualization, and reporting is not part of data mining.

Common techniques

Some of the most common and widely accepted and used data mining (statistical) analysis methods are explained in the following sub-sections.

Visualization

Visualization of averages, measures of variation, counts, percentages, cross-tabbing, and simple correlations help the data scientists in understanding the structure of the data. This is also referred to as **data profiling**.

 Area, temporal, multidimensional, and hierarchical are typical, commonly used, and easily understood formats for data visualization.

Cluster analysis

Cluster analysis is used by the data scientists to place data variables into defined collections (that is, clusters) as a way of summarizing the data. Clusters should be both internally homogeneous (the variables are like one another) as well as externally heterogeneous (the variables are not like members of other clusters).

 Hierarchical agglomerative, partitioning, and model-based are all very common methods of cluster analysis.

Correlation analysis

Correlation analysis is a method where the data scientists measure the relationship between two data variables. This results in something called a **correlation coefficient**, which shows if changes to one variable (the independent variable) will result in changes to the other (the dependent variable).

 Common correlation approaches are positive/negative and linear and non-linear.

Discriminant analysis

Discriminant analysis is used when there is no obvious natural ordering of groups to determine if a data variable is a member. With this method, there are predetermined groups with specific scores or measures that are used in the classification or grouping of the data variables process.

 Linear discriminant analysis (LDA) is one of the most common approaches to discriminate analysis where the data scientist attempts to find a linear combination of features that characterize or separates a data variable (into groups).

Factor analysis

Factor analysis is useful for understanding the reasons for the associations (amongst a group of data variables). The main goal is to try and reduce the number of variables and to detect structure in the relationships among them (this method also results in an overall data reduction).

 Types of factor analysis used by data scientists are the principal component, common, image, alpha, and factor regression.

Regression analysis

Regression analysis uses the relationship between two or more quantitative variables so that one variable (dependent variable) can be predicted from the other(s) (independent variables).

 There are many kinds of regression analysis, including simple linear, multiple linear, curvilinear, and multiple curvilinear, as well as logistic regression models.

Logistic analysis

A logistic analysis is a method that is used when the response variable is binary or qualitative and attempts to find a best fitting equation using a maximum likelihood method to maximize the probability of obtaining the observed results given the fitted regression coefficients.

 Some of the common flavours that logistic regression comes in include simple, multiple, polytomous, and Poisson logistic regression models.

Purpose

Through the practice of data mining, a data scientist can achieve (the aforementioned) goal of deriving actionable information from long information or data.

Some have said that the objective of data mining is to discover structure inside unstructured (data). For example, you might use data mining to identify customer segments to design a promotion targeting high-value customers or an inventory control plan to ensure short product shelf life.

One might confuse data querying with data mining. But if we consider the example of generating a plan for controlling inventory at a newly opened home improvement store, then by simply querying sales transactions to determine the fastest selling products from the past few months (from other store locations), we might not be successful. Mining demographical information might, however, yield better results, as we might identify valid novel, potentially useful, and understandable correlations and patterns in the data, which can then be used to predict local consumer purchasing. In other words, the objective or purpose of data mining is not reporting but uncovering.

In the next section, we'll take a closer look at the differences between data mining and data querying.

Mining versus querying

Data querying is the process of asking specific, structured questions of data in search of a specific answer, while data mining is the process of sifting through data to identify patterns and relationships using statistical algorithms.

The following matrix may help the data developers in gaining an understanding of the differences between data querying and data mining:

Example	Data querying or mining
What was the total number of technical books sold last month worldwide?	Data querying
What factors affected the type of technical books sold worldwide last month?	Data mining
How many different technologies' technical books were sold last quarter?	Data querying
Which technologies were purchased as part of a set?	Data mining
Does a technology tend to be purchased in hardcopy or electronic version?	Data mining
Which technical books have repeat customers?	Data mining
Which is the most sold technical book overall?	Data querying

Once again, data querying is about reporting the results of events while data mining is the process of identifying relationships that may help to understand which factors affected the outcome of those events, or they may be used to predict future outcomes of similar events.

Choosing R for data mining

Although there are many good options to choose from, R is a language and environment that has a short learning curve, is very flexible in nature, and is also very focused on statistical computing, making it great for manipulating, cleaning, summarizing, producing probability statistics, and so on (as well as actually creating visualizations with your data); thus, it's a great choice for the exercises data mining.

In addition, here are a few more reasons to learn and use R for data mining projects:

- R is used by a large number of academic statisticians, so it's a tool that is not going away
- R is pretty much platform independent; what you develop will run almost anywhere
- R has awesome help resources. Just google it and you'll see!

To illustrate, we'll explore a few practical data mining examples using the R programming language throughout the rest of this chapter.

Visualizations

To begin, let's look at creating a simple visualization of our data, using R. In this use case scenario, we have data collected from a theoretical hospital, whereupon admission, patient medical history information is collected through an online survey. Information is also added to a patient's file as treatment is provided. The file includes many fields, including:

- Basic descriptive data for the patient, such as sex, date of birth, height, weight, blood type, and so on
- Vital statistics, such as blood pressure, heart rate, and so on
- Medical history, such as number of hospital visits, surgeries, major illnesses or conditions, is currently under a doctor's care, and so on
- Demographical statistics, such as occupation, home state, educational background, and so on
- Some additional information is also collected in the file to develop patient characteristics and habits, such as the number of times the patient included beef, pork, and fowl in his or her weekly diet, if he or she typically uses a butter replacement product, and so on

Assuming we have been given no further information about the data (other than a brief field name list and the knowledge that the data is captured by hospital personnel upon patient admission), the next step would be to perform some data mining, that is identifying or grouping data and perhaps locating relationships between the variables.

To get started, we can read out hospital survey data into an R data frame and then use two available R functions to reveal information about our file:

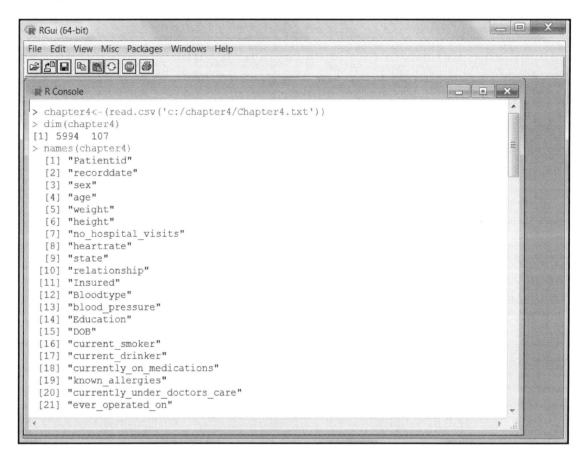

The code shown here reads our text file (named `Chapter4.txt`) into an R data frame (also named `chapter4`) and then uses the functions `dim` and `names`. The `dim` function shows us the file's data structure (there are `5994` records or cases in this file and `107` data points or variables, as shown in the screenshot we just saw). The `names` function simply lists all the field or variable names in our file (partially shown in the screenshot we just saw).

 R function attributes and `str` are also some very useful R data mining functions and would be worth the readers' time to investigate and experiment with further.

Initially, a data scientist might begin by looking through the field names for some ideas to start with; perhaps the common groups, such as sex, age, and state (insured is also a pretty interesting attribute these days!).

Current smokers

Often, a data scientist has an objective in mind when performing data mining. So in this example, let's suppose we are interested in grouping patients who are smokers into age groups. Using the variable `current_smoker`, we can use the R table function and run the following code:

```
table(chapter4["current_smoker"])
```

This yields the following information:

```
> table(chapter4["current_smoker"])

  No   Yes
5466   528
> |
```

From the results shown here, it seems like we have more non-smokers (`5466`) than smokers (`528`), at least in this file or population.

Next, what we'd like to see (that is, visualize) is the smoker patients in our population organized into (or by) age groups. To do this, a logical next step as a data scientist would be to understand the `range` of values present in the `age` variable. In other words, part of our data mining effort will be to see the age of the youngest patient, as well as the age of the oldest patient, within our population. Rather than having to slice and dice the data to find this information, we can use the R range function, as shown in the following screenshot:

```
> range(Chapter4["age"])
[1]  1 99
> |
```

From these results, the data scientist can now see that we have cases with patient ages ranging from 1 to 99 years! Another good idea would be to visualize the frequency of the ages of our patients. The data scientist might want to again use the R table function to create a histogram:

```
hist(table(Chapter4["age"]))
```

The output of the preceding code is:

```
> Chapter4<-read.csv('c:/chapter4/Chapter4.txt')
> hist(table(Chapter4["age"]))
> |
```

This R code will generate the following visualization, which provides, even more, visibility to our patients' ages:

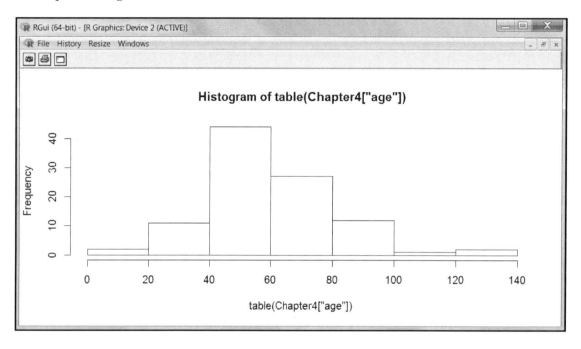

Another interesting bit of information is density estimation. Without much effort, we can nest the three R functions, `plot`, `density`, and `table`, to create another visual of patient age.

We can run the following code:

```
> plot(density(table(Chapter4["age"])))
> |
```

This will generate the following visualization:

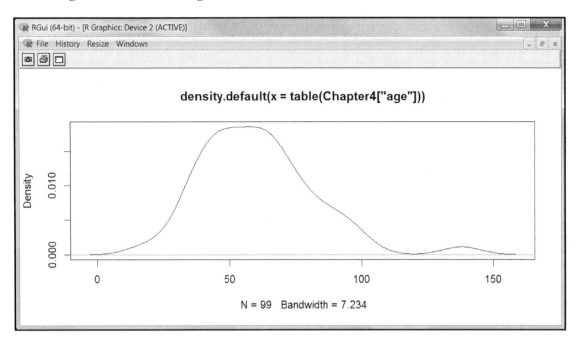

Given all this new-found knowledge, perhaps the data scientist will want to go ahead and group our cases into six distinct age groups:

- Under 22
- 22 to 34
- 35 to 44
- 45 to 54
- 55 to 64
- 65 and older

 To begin speaking the language of the data scientist, the data developer should start using the word cases rather than records (in the file) and population rather than the file.

The following R program code groups our cases into current smokers by their recorded age and then creates a simple pie chart to visualize the results:

```
# -- read our data into a data frame object
Chapter4<-read.csv('c:/chapter4/Chapter4.txt')

# -- initialize holders for counting cases
a1 <-0;a2 <-0;a3 <-0;a4 <-0;a5 <-0;a6 <-0
# -- read through the cases and count smokers by age group
for(i in 2:nrow(Chapter4))
{
if (as.numeric(Chapter4[i,"age"]) < 22 &
Chapter4[i,"current_smoker"]=="Yes") {a1 <- a1 + 1}
if (as.numeric(Chapter4[i,"age"]) > 21 & as.numeric(Chapter4[i,"age"]) < 35
& Chapter4[i,"current_smoker"]=="Yes") {a2 <- a2 + 1}
if (as.numeric(Chapter4[i,"age"]) > 34 & as.numeric(Chapter4[i,"age"]) < 45
& Chapter4[i,"current_smoker"]=="Yes") {a3 <- a3 + 1}
if (as.numeric(Chapter4[i,"age"]) > 44 & as.numeric(Chapter4[i,"age"]) < 55
& Chapter4[i,"current_smoker"]=="Yes") {a4 <- a4 + 1}
if (as.numeric(Chapter4[i,"age"]) > 54 & as.numeric(Chapter4[i,"age"]) < 65
& Chapter4[i,"current_smoker"]=="Yes") {a5 <- a5 + 1}
if (as.numeric(Chapter4[i,"age"]) > 64) {a6 <- a6 + 1}
}

# -- build a pie chart
slices <- c(a1, a2, a3, a4, a5, a6)
lbls <- c("under 21", "22-34","35-44","45-54","55-64", "65 & over")

# -- create the actual visualization
pie(slices, labels = lbls, main="Smokers by Age Range")
```

The following is our simple pie chart generated by using the R pie function:

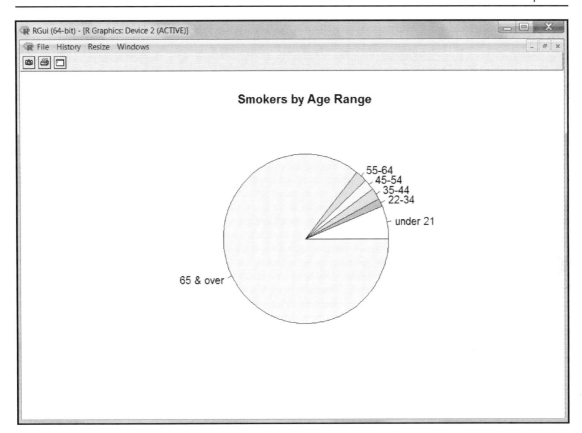

Missing values

Critical to the outcome of any analysis is the availability of data.

Suppose there are cases within our population that have values that are missing. You may want to ignore (or omit) those cases in your analysis. Rather than spending time writing code to deal with these cases, you can use the handy R generic function `na`. The `na.omit` function evaluates each case in your file and if it is missing any values for any of the variables, it drops that case automatically.

The following example shows the use of the R functions `na.omit` and `nrow` on a file with missing values:

```
> Chapter4<-read.csv('c:/chapter4/Chapter4_NA.csv')
> nrow(Chapter4)
[1] 5994
> Chapter4<-na.omit(Chapter4)
> nrow(Chapter4)
[1] 5988
>
```

Note the row (case) count before and after the use of `na.omit` (five records were dropped).

 I've overwritten the object `Chapter4` with the updated file; in reality, it is a good habit to create a new object so that you have an audit of your data before and after any processing.

A cluster analysis

In this next example, the data scientist wants to take a closer look at our cases, but only those that are smokers. So, with R, let's first create a subset of our original cases, including only those cases that are current smokers. As we did in the previous example, after we create our subset (named `mysub`), we will use the R `nrow` function to verify the number of records in our new population, so that we can get an idea of the number of cases in our new population:

```
# --- create a subset of smokers only cases
mysub <- subset(Chapter4,Chapter4["current_smoker"]=="Yes")

# --- confirm the row count
nrow(mysub)
```

The output of the preceding code is:

```
> # --- create a subset of smokers only
> mysub <- subset(Chapter4,Chapter4["current_smoker"]=="Yes")
> # --- confirm row count
> nrow(mysub)
[1] 528
>
```

As per the output we just saw, there are still over 500 cases in our new population. So, as a data scientist, we make the decision to pull a random sample of our cases (which we will then perform a cluster analysis on) and then, again, validate the number of records in our newest population.

We can use the R `sample` command to create a sample of just 30 cases:

```
# --- create a random sample of 30 smokers
mysample <- mysub[sample(1:nrow(mysub), 30,
    replace=FALSE),]
# --- confirm the row count in our random case sample
nrow(mysample)
```

The output of the preceding code is:

```
> # --- create a random sample of 30 smokers
> mysample <- mysub[sample(1:nrow(mysub), 30,
+     replace=FALSE),]
> # --- confirm the row count in our sample
> nrow(mysample)
[1] 30
>
```

Finally, our data scientist feels that he now has a small enough sampling of our cases that is easy enough to work with, so let's go ahead and perform a cluster analysis with it. As mentioned earlier in this chapter, hierarchical agglomerative is one of the most popular cluster analysis techniques, and so we will use it with our random sample of cases.

We can perform the hierarchical agglomerative cluster analysis of our random sample of cases using a combination of the R's `dist` and `hclust` functions. The `dist` function calculates a distance matrix for your dataset, giving the Euclidean distance between any two observations. The `hclust` function performs hierarchical clustering on that distance matrix.

In conclusion, the easiest way to review and understand the results of a hierarchical cluster analysis is through visualization of the results. This visualization is known as a **dendrogram** (a tree diagram frequently used to illustrate the arrangement of the clusters), so we'll add that code as well:

```
# -- perform the hierarchical cluster analysis
smokerclust<-hclust(dist(mysample))

# -- create results in a dendrogram
plot(smokerclust)
```

The output of the preceding code is:

```
> # -- perform hierarchical cluster
> smokerclust<-hclust(dist(mysample))
> # -- create results in a dendrogram
> plot(smokerclust)
>
```

This code sample creates the following visualization:

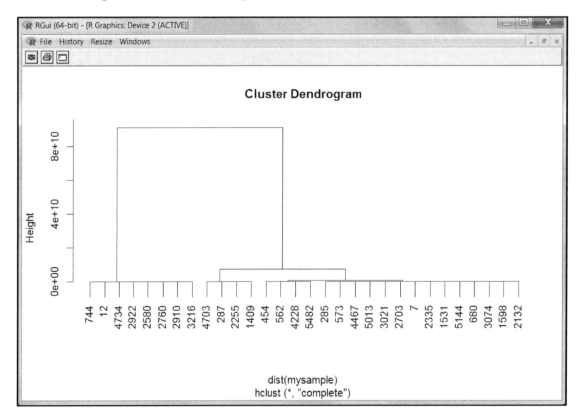

 R offers a long list of options for creating rich visualizations based upon data and statistics. It is important for a data scientist to be familiar with these options and, perhaps more importantly, understand which type of visualization best fits the objective of the analysis.

Dimensional reduction

Clustering is intended to group data variables that are found to be interrelated, based on observations of their attributes' values. However, given a scenario with a large number of attributes, the data scientist will find that some of the attributes will usually not be meaningful for a given cluster. In the example, we used earlier in this chapter (dealing with patient cases), we could have found this situation. Recall that we performed a hierarchical cluster analysis on smokers only. Those cases include many attributes, such as, sex, age, weight, height, no_hospital_visits, heartrate, state, relationship, Insurance blood type, blood_pressure, education, date of birth, current_drinker, currently_on_medications, known_allergies, currently_under_doctors_care, ever_operated_on, occupation, heart_attack, rheumatic_fever, heart_murmur, diseases_of_the_arteries, and so on.

As a data scientist, you can use the R function `names`, as we did earlier in this chapter, to see the complete list of attributes.

Dimensional reduction is a process where the data scientist attempts to reduce or limit the number of attributes, or dimensions, within a case. This is referred to as reducing the number of random variables under consideration, but what that translates to is simply removing columns from a data file, based upon scientific theory.

Currently accepted and commonly used approaches to eliminating dimensions include:

- Missing data: If a variable (column) has many cases (records) with no values, it is not going to add much value; therefore, the column can be removed.
- Remember, earlier in this chapter, we used the R function `na.omit`. This function comes in handy for removing entire cases; however, with dimensional reduction, we want to omit the entire variable for all cases.
- Little variance: Like a variable having a great number of missing values, variables with little variation do not add value and can be removed.
- High correlation: Data columns with very similar trends are also likely to carry very similar information. In this case, only one of them is needed.
- Decision trees: It is a technique that may require a bit more work. It is an approach to dimensionality reduction where the data scientist generates a set of decision trees against a target attribute and then uses each attribute's usage statistics to find the most informative features (or columns). The columns with the lowest statistics may be dropped.

- **Principal component analysis (PCA)**: It is a process that transforms variables in a dataset into a new set of variables called **principal components**. The components are ordered by the variables' possible variance and only those with the highest variance are kept.
- Backward elimination and forward construction: These techniques involve focusing on one or more variables, and sequentially removing or adding one additional variable at a time and observing the effect. Backward elimination measures effect with a tolerable error rate, while forward construction measures by the effect on performance.

Calculating statistical significance

Let's now look at a simple example of using a data variables calculated variance to determine if it should be removed from an analysis.

Again, using our same patient cases example that we've used throughout this chapter, we can use the R function `var` to determine the statistical significance of the variables within our population.

 The R function `var` only works with numeric values.

In the next code, we use the R `var` function to calculate the variance of the variable named:

```
"no_servings_per_week_skim_milk".
```

We can see that it has a low variance percentage (it doesn't vary often or is not found to have many different values, case by case):

```
> Chapter4<-read.csv('c:/chapter4/varainces.csv')
> var(Chapter4["No_servings_per_week_skim_milk"])
                                    No_servings_per_week_skim_milk
No_servings_per_week_skim_milk                         0.003160316
>
```

If we look at the calculated variance percentage of yet another variable, this one named: No_servings_per_week_regular_or_diet_soda, we see that it has a higher calculated variance (than the previous variable):

```
> Chapter4<-read.csv('c:/chapter4/varainces.csv')
> var(Chapter4["No_servings_per_week_skim_milk"])
                            No_servings_per_week_skim_milk
No_servings_per_week_skim_milk            0.003160316
> var(Chapter4["No_servings_per_week_regular_or_diet_soda"])
                                No_servings_per_week_regular_or_diet_soda
No_servings_per_week_regular_or_diet_soda                        8.505655
>
```

And finally, if we look at a third variable, this one named No_servings_per_week_water, we get a third calculated variance:

```
> var(Chapter4["No_servings_per_week_water"])
                            No_servings_per_week_water
No_servings_per_week_water                   24.10477
>
```

From these individual variance calculations, we can see how statistically significant each of these variables may be in our case analysis:

Data Variable	Calculated Variance
No_servings_per_week_skim_milk	.003160316
No_servings_per_week_regular_or_diet_soda	8.505655
No_servings_per_week_water	24.10477

The data variable named No_servings_per_week_skim_milk could be certainly eliminated from the analysis, and depending upon our data scientists tolerance levels, possibly the data variable named No_servings_per_week_regular_or_diet_soda could be eliminated from our analysis as well.

Using simple R functions, we can visualize our calculated variance data for a better understanding:

```
> Chapter4<-read.csv('c:/chapter4/varainces.csv')
> c1<-var(Chapter4["No_servings_per_week_skim_milk"])
> c2<-var(Chapter4["No_servings_per_week_regular_or_diet_soda"])
> c3<-var(Chapter4["No_servings_per_week_water"])
> variances<-c(c1, c2, c3)
> plot(variances, pch=16, col="green")
> lines(variances, col="blue")
> |
```

So, we generate the following visualization:

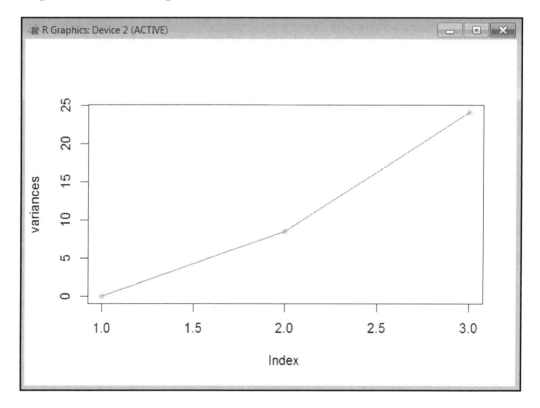

 When we eliminate a variable, it is eliminated from all cases within our population.

Frequent patterning

To gain an understanding of statistical patterning, let us begin with thinking about what happens when an urban area is threatened by severe weather and potentially hazardous traveling—all the local stores sell out of bread, milk, and eggs!

Patterning (which is a subfield of data mining) is the process of looking through data in an effort to identify previously unknown but potentially useful patterns consisting of frequently co-occurring events (such as the stormy weather event triggering the sale of bread, milk, and eggs) or objects (such as the products bread, milk, and eggs being typically purchased together or bundled together in the same shopping cart).

Pattern mining is the process that consists of using or developing custom pattern mining logic. This logic might be applied to various types of data sources (such as transaction and sequence databases, streams, strings, spatial data, graphs, and so on) in an effort to look for various types of patterns.

At a higher level, data scientists look for:

- Interesting patterns
- Frequent patterns
- Rare patterns
- Patterns with a high confidence
- The top patterns, and others

Some of the more specific types of patterns that may exist in data include:

- **Subgraphs**: The discovery of an interesting graph(s) within a graph or in a set of graphs
- **Direct and indirect associations**: Identifying couplings or dependencies between objects or events; either implicit or explicit defined
- **Trends**: This is also sometimes known as trend analysis, and is the practice of collecting seemingly unrelated information and attempting to spot a pattern
- **Periodic patterns**: This is defined as a trend or change in the character of an element, either across a period or group
- **Sequential rules**: This is an add-on to sequential pattern mining, taking into account the probability that an identified pattern will be followed
- **Lattices**: A partially ordered set in which every two elements have a unique least upper bound and a unique greatest lower bound

- **Sequential patterns**: A subsequence that appears in several sequences of a data
- **High-utility patterns**: High utility patterns are those patterns that have been determined to have higher, greater, or equal to a threshold value

Frequent item-setting

Building on the idea in the previous section (of finding frequent patterns) is frequent item-setting. To the data developer, by far the most applicable patterning concept is that of frequent item-setting or finding items that are found to be frequently a member of a group or set.

Using our stormy weather example from earlier in this chapter, one can envision the process of searching through a file or database of sales transactions, looking for the occasion (that is, the event) where milk, bread, and eggs were purchased together as one sale (or one set of products).

Frequent item setting also involves determining a minsup or minimum supported threshold to be used within an analysis. What this means is that the data scientist will determine the minimum occurrence of items that constitute a set.

Again, going back to our stormy weather example, if the data scientist sets a minsup of two to be used, then sales, where just two of the member products exist, would be considered a set or pattern.

Let us consider the following sales transactions:

Sales ID	Items Purchased	Qualifies (as a Frequent Item set)
Sale 1	Milk, Bread, Eggs	Yes
Sale 2	Milk, Potatoes	No
Sale 3	Bread, Eggs, Tea	Yes
Sale 4	Eggs, Orange Juice	No

 The most known algorithm for pattern mining, without a doubt, is Apriori, designed to be applied to a transaction database to discover patterns in transactions made by customers in stores. This algorithm takes as input a minsup threshold set by the user and a transaction database containing a set of transactions and outputs all the frequent item-sets.

Sequence mining

Sequence mining evolves the preceding concepts even further. This is a process that the data scientist uses to discover a set of patterns that are shared among objects but which also have between them a specific order.

With sequence mining, we acknowledge that there are sequence rules associated with identified sequences. These rules define the pattern's objects and order. A sequence can have multiple rules. The support of a sequence rule can be calculated or determined by the data scientist by the number of sequences containing the rule divided by the total number of sequences. The confidence of a sequence rule will be the number of sequences containing the rule divided by the number of sequences containing its antecedent.

Overall, the objective of sequential rule mining is to discover all sequential rules having a support and confidence no less than two thresholds, given by the user named minsup and minconf.

Summary

In this chapter, we provided a universal definition for data mining, listed the most common techniques used by data scientists, and stated the overall objective of the efforts. Data mining was also compared to data querying and, using R, various working examples were given to illustrate certain key techniques. Finally, the concepts of dimensional reduction, frequent patterning, and sequence mining were explored.

The next chapter will be a hands-on introduction to statistical analysis of data through the eyes of a data developer, providing instructions for describing the nature of data, exploring relationships presented in data, creating a summarization model from data, proving the validly of a data model, and employing predictive analytics on a data developed model.

5

Statistical Analysis for the Database Developer

This chapter introduces the data developer to the practice of statistical analysis.

As a data developer, the concept or process of data analysis may be clear to your mind. However, although there happen to be similarities between the art of data analysis and that of statistical analysis, there are important differences to be understood as well.

In this chapter, we aim to point to both the similarities and differences between the types of analysis, helping the reader understand the fundamental principles of the processes of data, summarization, and statistical analysis that describe the key factors or characteristics found in a successful statistical analysis effort, and provide working examples of each step required in successful statistical analysis of data.

In this chapter, we've broken things into the following topics:

- What are data analysis, statistical analysis, and summarization?
- The steps in successful statistical analysis of data
- Using R for statistical analysis of data
- Examples--a summarization model

Data analysis

Let's start by looking at what is known as **data analysis**. This is defined as a structured process undertaken to evaluate data using analytical and logical reasoning. One performs data analysis by taking the time to gather up all the data to be analyzed, breaking that data (now viewed as a data source) into chunks or components (that can be reviewed), and then drawing a conclusion based upon what is seen or found within the data. Typically, this is done in an effort to determine that a data source is useable for meeting a declared project deliverable.

There are a variety of specific data analysis approaches, some of which include data mining (discussed in `Chapter 4`, *Data Mining and the Database Developer*), text analytics, business intelligence, and data visualizations (just to name a few of them).

To a data developer, data analysis involves inspecting the individual parts of a data source with an intention in mind.

For example, suppose we have some transactional data collected from a bicycle manufacturing organization, that we want to potentially use for a sales performance reporting deliverable. Typical of these types of projects, let us say that we've been supplied data extracted from a database in CSV format.

Now, using R commands, we can identify the fields or columns in the data as well as view a summarization. The following R code uses `read.csv` to load our data file into an R data frame object, and then the command `colnames` to list the field or column names found within our file; then, we finally use the R command summary to instruct R to provide us with some statistics on our data.

The following screenshot shows the output of running the R commands (`colnames` and `summary`):

```
> myData <-read.csv("c:/Worker/SamplesSalesTrans.csv")
> colnames(myData)
[1] "product_code" "product_name" "quantity"     "sales_date"   "return_date"  "sales_region"
> summary(myData)
  product_code       product_name      quantity         sales_date        return_date       sales_region
 Min.   : 1.0    Bell      : 19    Min.   :   2               :129                :911    Min.   :1.00
 1st Qu.:25.0    Rack      : 19    1st Qu.:2469    2/16/2013: 25    1/22/2013:  9    1st Qu.:2.00
 Median :51.0    Head badge: 18    Median :5040    1/17/2013: 22    1/9/2013 :  5    Median :3.00
 Mean   :50.4    Locknut   : 17    Mean   :5073    1/18/2013: 22    2/22/2013:  5    Mean   :2.99
 3rd Qu.:75.0    Cable     : 16    3rd Qu.:7653    1/9/2013 : 22    2/24/2013:  5    3rd Qu.:4.00
 Max.   :99.0    Chainguard: 16    Max.   :9983    2/3/2013 : 20    1/2/2013 :  4    Max.   :5.00
                 (Other)   :935                    (Other)  :800    (Other)  :101
> |
```

Looking closer

Once we've established that our data includes product identifiers (numbers and names), a transactional quantity, a sales date, a return date, sales region information, and so on, we will want to do some explorations (analysis) of the components found in the data. Perhaps, we can start this effort by establishing the total number of records in our file, using the R command nrow, then list the unique part or product numbers present within our data, using the R commands list and unique, as shown in the following code and partial output:

```
> nrow(myData)
[1] 1040
> list(unique(myData$product_name))
[[1]]
 [1] Freehub
 [2] Seat lug
 [3] Handlebar plug
 [4] Handlebar tape
 [5] Locknut
 [6] Kickstand
```

Further data analysis tasks would include examining each of the components found in the data, for example:

- What is the format of the date values found in the sales_date and return_date (components) fields?
- What is the range of dates within these fields?
- How many unique products and sales regions are included in our data file?

Keep in mind that dates are always tricky, so determining the format and range is always a valuable analysis exercise to perform in any data analysis that contains date or time values.

To illustrate, let us use a few simple R commands to create a list of the years and the months found in our data.

The following is the R code used to accomplish this statistical analysis task:

```
# --- read our data file into "x"
x <-read.table("c:/Worker/23SamplesSalesTrans.csv", sep=",", header = 
FALSE, skip = 1)
# --- convert "x" into a data frame object, then set the data frame to
# --- hold only the sales_date
data.df <- data.frame(x)
```

```
data.df <- data.df[,4]
# --- use the R commands substr and regexpr to strip out just the year and
# --- month from the sales date field
YearsInData = substr(substr(data.df[], (regexpr('/',data.df[])+1),11), (
regexpr('/',substr(data.df[], (regexpr('/',data.df[])+1),11))+1),11)
MonthsInData = substr(data.df[], (regexpr('/',data.df[])-1),1)
# --- use sort and unique functions to list our year(s) and month(s)
sort(unique(YearsInData))
sort(unique(MonthsInData))
```

The following screenshot shows the output from running the previous commands:

```
> # --- use sort and unique functions to list our year(s) and month(s)
>
> sort(unique(YearsInData))
[1] ""       "2013"
> sort(unique(MonthsInData))
[1] ""   "1" "2" "3"
>
```

We can see that our data contains information only for the first quarter, months 1, 2, and 3 of the calendar year 2013. Now we have established our data's time series. There's still plenty of data analysis work that can be done, but the point is that we're performing analysis exercises aimed at establishing structure so that we can meet our original objective of sales performance reporting, rather than any machine learning.

With this in mind, let us suppose we want to examine what the transaction volumes are by month. To do that, we can use R to calculate these monthly totals using the following R code:

```
# --- read data
data.df<-data.frame(x)
# --- initialize counters
JanuarySales <-0
FebruarySales <-0
MarchSales <-0
# --- loop and count
for(i in 1:nrow(data.df))
{
    MonthInData = substr(data.df[i,4], (regexpr('/',data.df[i,4])-1),1)
if (MonthInData == '1') {JanuarySales <- JanuarySales + data.df[i,3]}
if (MonthInData == '2') {FebruarySales <- FebruarySales + + data.df[i,3]}
if (MonthInData == '3') {MarchSales <- MarchSales + + data.df[i,3]}
}
```

Once we have our monthly transaction totals calculated (using the preceding commands), we can then report those results. This can be done by creating a simple bar chart visualization.

We can use the R `barplot` function in the following code:

```
barplot(c(JanuarySales, FebruarySales, MarchSales), main="Sales Qty by
Month", border = "dark blue", legend.text = c("Jan", "Feb", "Mar"), col =
c("lightblue", "mistyrose","lightcyan"), sub = "Sales Transactions from
File")
```

The preceding command generates the following visualization:

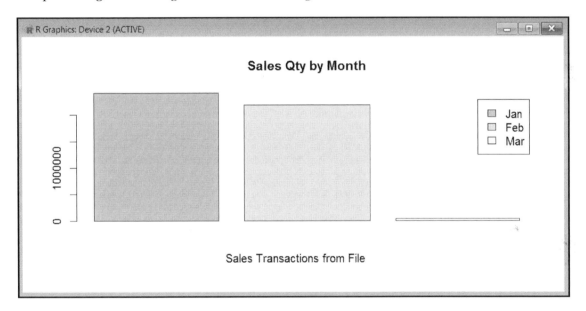

These described examples of data analysis tasks are just a few of the many steps that are typically completed when conducting data analysis work focused on a particular objective, such as delivering performance reports.

To sum up, data analysis is about reviewing data to determine if it can be a valid source for creating a selected result, and, if so, how it can be used.

Next, let's move on to statistical analysis in the next section.

Statistical analysis

Some in the study of statistics sometimes describe statistical analysis as part of statistical projects that involves the collection and scrutiny of a data source in an effort to identify trends within the data.

With data analysis, the goal is to validate that the data is appropriate for a need, and with statistical analysis, the goal is to make sense of, and draw some inferences from, the data.

There is a wide range of possible statistical analysis techniques or approaches that can be considered.

Summarization

Let's return to our bicycle parts manufacturing organization example. Suppose we have a new file of transactions and this time we have more data and our efforts are going to be focused on performing a statistical analysis with the intention of identifying specifics that may be contributing to the sales performance reported as part of the preceding activities.

Step one a summarization of the data. The previous section already presented some groupings: products and periods. Using those components, we were able to be telling the story of the organization's sales performance.

What other groupings or categories might be within the data?

For example, if we theorize that sales performance is dependent upon a period of time, the first thing to do is probably to group the data into time periods. Standard time periods are, of course, month, quarter, and year (and we already did that in a prior section), but statistically speaking, the more data the better, so a better time grouping might be ten or five-year chunks.

A common practice used during summarization is visualization, typically with bar charts, which show every data point in order, or histograms, which are bar charts grouped into broader categories. In this section, we'll keep this in mind and use R to create various visualizations to illustrate the results of our data summarizations.

Comparing groups

Let's go ahead and (like we did previously in this chapter) use the R commands `colnames` and `summary`; this time on our new data file:

```
> x <-read.csv("c:/Worker/SamplesSalesTrans_2.csv", sep=",", header = TRUE, skip = 0)
> colnames(x)
[1] "product_code" "product_name" "quantity"    "sales_date"  "return_date" "sales_region" "sale_type"
> |
```

As can be seen, there is an additional field (or component) present in our file, sale_type, and executing the summary command yields the following statistics, including a breakdown of the sale types:

```
> summary(x)
  product_code
Min.   : 1.00
1st Qu.:25.50
Median :50.00
Mean   :49.55
3rd Qu.:74.00
Max.   :99.00


Gusset
Bicycle brake cable
Cup
Dustcap
1) the disc component of a disc brake.[1]2) another name for a detangler - a device that allows the handlebars and
Bar ends
(Other)
   quantity       sales_date      return_date     sales_region         sale_type
Min.   :  10    : 279         :1960    Min.   :1.000    Vendor       :296
1st Qu.:2590   1/22/2014:  27   2/2/2014 :   7   1st Qu.:2.000   Club        :288
Median :5122   2/27/2013:  27   1/7/2014 :   6   Median :3.000   Repeat      :287
Mean   :5044   2/12/2014:  26   2/14/2014:   6   Mean   :2.995   Online      :285
3rd Qu.:7480   1/3/2014 :  24   2/15/2014:   6   3rd Qu.:4.000   Retailer    :284
Max.   :9986   2/2/2013 :  24   2/17/2014:   6   Max.   :5.000   New Customer:276
               (Other)  :1832   (Other)  : 248                  (Other)     :523
> |
```

The next step will depend on your hypothesis. If, for example, you have some idea that the type of sale (sale_type) has some effect on the overall sales performance, you then need to produce the summary data for each (sales type) group, usually mean, median, and/or standard deviation (the preceding summary command was a good start). Let's see some examples of using R to create this summary information.

As always, we can first readout data into R and then explicitly move it into an R data frame object. The following code works for this step:

```
# --- read in the data in
sales <- read.csv("c:/Worker/SamplesSalesTrans_2.csv")
# --- just moving our original data to a data frame object
# --- preserving the original
data.df<-data.frame(sales.new)
```

There are many different ways or approaches to accomplish the same things when using the R language but, in this example, we'll use the most straightforward, simplest approach of looping through the data, creating summary totals of each sale type.

The following is the looping code we use:

```
# --- looping through the data and counting quantities
# --- type
for(i in 1:nrow(data.df))
{
if (data.df[i,2] == 'Online')
   {Online <- Online + data.df[i,1]
         OnlineC <- OnlineC +1}
if (data.df[i,2] == 'Television')
   {Television <- Television + data.df[i,1]
   TelevisionC <- TelevisionC +1}
if (data.df[i,2] == 'New Customer')
   {NewCustomer <- NewCustomer + data.df[i,1]
   NewCustomerC <- NewCustomerC +1}
if (data.df[i,2] == 'Retailer')
   {Retailer <- Retailer + data.df[i,1]
   RetailerC <- RetailerC +1}
if (data.df[i,2] == 'Club')
   {Club <- Club + data.df[i,1]
   ClubC <- ClubC +1}
if (data.df[i,2] == 'Discounted')
   {Discounted <- Discounted + data.df[i,1]
   DiscountedC <- DiscountedC +1}
if (data.df[i,2] == 'Repeat')
   {Repeat <- Repeat + data.df[i,1]
   RepeatC <- RepeatC +1}
if (data.df[i,2] == 'Vendor')
   {Vendor <- Vendor + data.df[i,1]
   VendorC <- VendorC +1}
}
```

A more efficient way, perhaps, is to create subsets of our data, in this case, by `sale_type`. This can be accomplished by using the following R commands:

```
# --- create average or mean for all Online sales quantities
# --- by first creating a subset of only quanities of that sale
# --- type
OnlineSales.new <-data.df[data.df$sale_type == "Online",]
OnlineSalesMean <-mean(OnlineSales.new$quantity)
# --- using the summary totals, you could do the math to calculate # ---
the average or mean:
OnlineMean <- Online/OnlineC
```

In addition, we can use the R functions mean, median and standard distribution to calculate statistical summary information on our data, shown in the R command as follows:

```
# --- calculate the mean for all sale types:
MeanAll <-mean(data.df [["quantity"]])
# --- calculate the standard deviation for all sales types:
StdDAll<-sd(data.df[["quantity"]])
# --- calculate the median for all sales types:
MeanAll <-mean(data.df [["quantity"]])
```

The following image shows the results of running the preceding commands:

```
> # --- mean for all sale types:
> MeanAll <-mean(data.df [["quantity"]])
>
> # --- standard deviation for all sales types:
> StdDAll<-sd(data.df[["quantity"]])
>
> # --- median for all sales types:
> MeanAll <-mean(data.df [["quantity"]])
> MeanAll
[1] 5043.971
> StdDAll
[1] 2876.796
> MeanAll
[1] 5043.971
> |
```

Once we have some summary information calculated, the next step is to create one or more visualizations using that information, so that we can observe and study it more easily.

A histogram is a nice visualization option for accomplishing this goal. We can use the R function hist once we perform a few more data manipulations, as noted in the following lines of R code:

```
# --- using the calculated average/mean for each sale type
temp<-c(Online, Television, NewCustomer, Retailer, Club, Discounted,
Repeat, Vendor)

# --- create the histogram
hist(temp, breaks=8, freq=TRUE, main="Quantity by Sales Type",
border="black", col = "gray", xlab="Types: Online, Televsion, New Customer,
Retailer, Club, Discounted, Repeat, Vendor")
abline(v=ref,col="red")
```

The following diagram shows the histogram visualization created by the preceding R commands:

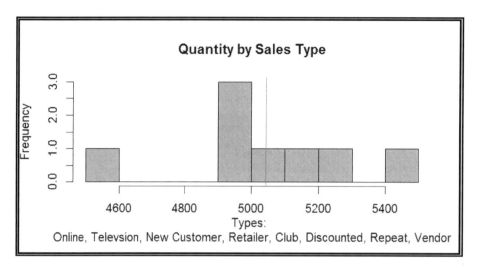

In order to decide whether there is a genuine difference between any of the observation groups, most times you would first establish a reference or a reference distribution against which to measure the values from each of the groups (in this case each `sales type` group).

The most common reference is standard distribution. Standard distribution measures variation, or how different and/or spread-out a set of values are; in this example, our `sales quantities`. As we did earlier in this section, we can use the R command `sd` to establish the standard distribution of all the products in our data source using the following R command:

```
# -- calculate standard distribution of all product quantities
sd(data.df[["quantity"]])
```

We can then do a quick visual to compare the `summary` data from each `sales type` group to our standard distribution.

The following R commands can be used to compute each group's standard distribution total:

```
# --- create a subset of only online sale type quantities
quantity.new <- data.df[data.df$sale_type == "Online",]

# --- calculate this subsets standard distribution
StdDOnline<-sd(quantity.new$quantity)
# --- repeated for each sales type group!
```

Then, we can plot the standard distribution totals for a visual comparison using the following R commands:

```
# --- after computing each type, calculate the standard
# --- distribution for all sales quantities:
StdDVendor<-sd(quantity.new$quantity)

# --- combine the totals into "Temp"
Temp<-c(StdDOnline, StdDTelevision, StdDNewCustomer, StdDRetailer,
StdDClub, StdDDiscounted, StdDRepeat, StdDVendor)

# --- create a simple Line Chart
plot(Temp, type="o", col="blue",    axes=FALSE, ann=FALSE)
axis(1, at=1:8, lab=c("Online", "TV","New",
"Retail","Club","Disc","Rep","Ven"))
title(ylab="STD DIST", col.lab=rgb(0,0.5,0))
box()
```

The following line chart visualization, showing plotted standard distributions for each sales type, is then generated from the preceding commands:

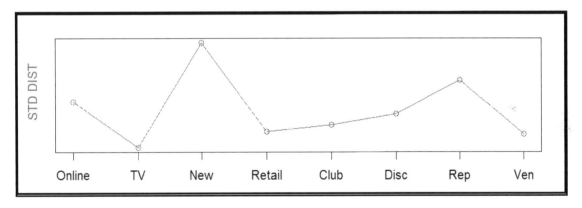

One thing we forgot to plot in this visualization is the standard distribution for all sales types. Using the previous calculation and the R abline function, we can update our visualization with the following R command:

```
abline(h=sd(data.df[["quantity"]]), col="green")
```

The following is our visualization updated with a horizontal line (green horizontal line) or watermark, depicting the standard distribution for all `sales types`:

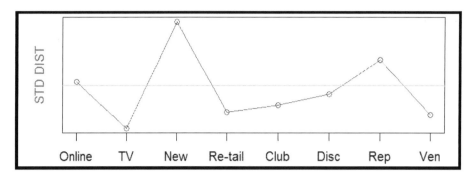

The preceding figure now gives us an idea of how each sales type compares to a standard distribution total.

Samples

Typically, you'd want to compare distributions to a sample (rather than a total of all the quantities), so we can use the R sample function to create a sample (sourced from our data):

```
# --- use sample to create a random sampling of data
mysample.df <- data.df[sample(1:nrow(data.df), 100, replace=FALSE),]
```

Then, we can recreate the previous visualization (using `plot`, `axis`, `title`, and `box`), with the horizontal line or watermark representing the (random) sample's standard distribution:

```
# --- original visualization
plot(Temp, type="o", col="blue",    axes=FALSE, ann=FALSE)
axis(1, at=1:8, lab=c("Online", "TV", "New",
"Retail","Club","Disc","Rep","Ven"))
title(ylab="STD DIST", col.lab=rgb(0,0.5,0))
box()

# --- create a sample population
mysample.df <- data.df[sample(1:nrow(data.df), 100, replace=FALSE),]

# --- draw a water mark from the
$ --- samples standard distribution
abline(h=sd(mysample.df[["quantity"]]), col="green")
```

Running the preceding R code creates the following visualization:

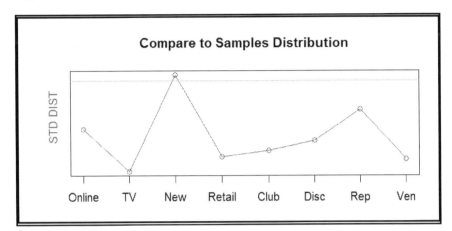

Other methods of comparing groups during statistical analysis include averaging, specifically mean, median, and mode.

Another key comparison is the measurement of spread, that is, how widely the data is spread across the whole possible measurement scale. Typically, we perform this analysis by calculating variances. Again, R makes this a straightforward task by using the `var` function.

The following commands calculate the variance for our sample, as well as for the entire population:

```
# --- calculate our samples variance
var(mysample.df[["quantity"]])

# --- calculate total variance
var(data.df[["quantity"]])
```

Group comparison conclusions

Before moving on, let's point out that you need to be careful of what conclusions you draw from your statistical analysis of groups. In the preceding example, we focused on comparing distributions. Using a single comparison point may cause you to make inaccurate assumptions, for example:

- The groups are different, but you conclude that they are not
- The groups are the same or very similar, but you conclude that they are different

To avoid these errors, it is wise to calculate and observe many summarization points within your data. To do this, you can create a summarization model, which is the topic covered in our next section.

Summarization modeling

The common practice of establishing multiple summarization points is through the development of a summation model. Simply put, to create a summarization model from the data is to create a table or data frame with the rows being mean, standard distribution, median, min, max, and a total for each component in the data (or at least each component in the data that you are interested in).

Let's use our previous data example, where we examined sales quantities by individual `sales type` group. Fortunately, R gives us simple functions to calculate our comparison points: max, mean, standard distribution, median, min, and sum.

We can use them to calculate each group's comparison points individually, as follows:

```
# --- create subset of Online quantities
quantity.new <- data.df[data.df$sale_type == "Online",]
# --- calculate each comparison point
max(quantity.new[["quantity"]])
mean(quantity.new[["quantity"]])
sd(quantity.new[["quantity"]])
median(quantity.new[["quantity"]])
min(quantity.new[["quantity"]])
sum(quantity.new[["quantity"]])
```

We next create an R `data frame` (`df`) object to hold our summarizations and then load all our comparison points into the data frame. This is done with the following lines of R code:

```
# --- create a data frame object for summarization
df<-data.frame(8,7)
# --- create our subset of data - this is online sales
quantity.new <- data.df[data.df$sale_type == "Online",]
# --- calculate comparison points based upon
# --- our current subset dropping each in a temp
# --- variable for now (a, b, c, d, e and f)
a<-max(quantity.new[["quantity"]])
b<-mean(quantity.new[["quantity"]])
c<-sd(quantity.new[["quantity"]])
d<-median(quantity.new[["quantity"]])
e<-min(quantity.new[["quantity"]])
f<-sum(quantity.new[["quantity"]])
# --- load our calculations into the data frame object
```

```
# --- just using "i" as an index to the data frame
i<-1
df[i,1]<-"Online"
df[i,2]<-a
df[i,3]<-b
df[i,4]<-c
df[i,5]<-d
df[i,6]<-e
df[i,7]<-f
# --- add headings/column names to our data frame object
names(df)<-c("group", "max", "mean", "sd", "median", "min", "sum")
# --- note: repeat the section of code here that creates a
# --- subset and calculates its points for all sale types
# --- display out finished summation model
df
```

Following is our summarization model data frame object example:

```
> df
            group   max      mean       sd median  min      sum
1          Online  9982  5160.888  2883.941  5100.0   33  1470853
2              TV  9970  4516.475  2803.657  4305.0   30  1151701
3    New Customer  9954  5052.507  2986.567  4966.5  122  1394492
4         Retailer  9986  4972.775  2832.253  4862.0   10  1412268
5            Club  9980  5282.920  2843.501  5560.5   30  1521481
6      Discounted  9918  5408.142  2862.614  5622.0   10  1449382
7          Repeat  9950  4937.014  2920.933  5068.0   90  1416923
8          Vendor  9848  4987.676  2827.729  5137.0   40  1476352
>
```

A *summary* table, such as the one we created previously, typically does not answer all of your questions about the data, but in fact, as it should, generates more questions and hypothesis for you to explore. Statistical analysis is about coming up with the next question to ask for the data.

Summary tables help us to determine:

- Is there really any significant message to be found within this data?
- Is this data source reliable?
- If this data appears to support my hypothesis, how strong is the evidence overall?
- Does this information (as summarized) really matter (to my current hypothesis)?
- What do these numbers mean (implying more analysis and summation may be needed)?

- What can next actions be taken from here?
- What is the nature of the data? (Discussed in the next section.)

 There are various R packages (such as the `gridExtra` package) available that can be downloaded and installed to print nicely formatted data frames to paper. It's worthy of the reader's time to explore some of these options.

Establishing the nature of data

When asked about the objectives of statistical analysis, one often refers to the process of describing or establishing the nature of a data source.

Establishing the nature of something implies gaining an understanding of it. This understanding can be found to be both simple as well as complex. For example, can we determine the types of each of the variables or components found within our data source; are they quantitative, comparative, or qualitative?

Using the example transactional data source used earlier in this chapter, we can identify some variables by types, as the following:

- Quantitative: quantity
- Comparative: `sale_type`
- Qualitative: `sales_region`
- Categorical: `product_name`

A more advanced statistical analysis aims to identify patterns in data; for example, whether there is a relationship between the variables or whether certain groups are more likely to show certain attributes than others.

 Exploring the relationships presented in data may appear to be similar to the idea of identifying a foreign key in a relational database, but in statistics, relationships between the components or variables are based upon correlation and causation.

Further, establishing the nature of a data source is also, really, a process of modeling that data source. During modeling, the process always involves asking questions such as the following (in an effort establish the nature of the data):

- What? Some common examples of this (what) are revenue, expenses, shipments, hospital visits, website clicks, and so on. In the example that we are using in this chapter, we are measuring quantities, that is, the amount of product that is being moved (sales).
- Why? This (why) will typically depend upon your project's specific objectives, which can vary immensely. For example, we may want to track the growth of a business, the activity on a website, or the evolution of a selected product or market interest. Again, in our current transactional data example, we may want to identify over- and under-performing `sales types`, and determine if, new or repeat customers provide more or fewer sales?
- How? The how will most likely be over a period of time (perhaps a year, month, week, and so on) and then by some other related measure, such as a product, state, region, reseller, and so on. Within our transactional data example, we've focused on the observation of quantities by sale type.

At the start of our discussion on data analysis in this chapter, we created a visualization showing the previously stated model, that is, quantities by month. Following is that visualization:

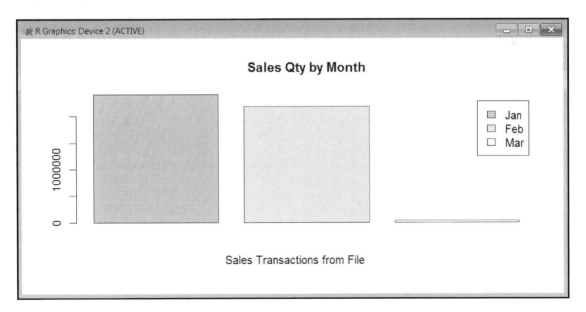

Typically, the modeling process will include multiple iterations of observing, asking new questions, manipulating the data, creating new visualizations, and observing those visualizations, with each iteration driven by the outcome(s) of the one before.

For example, after viewing the preceding visualization (sales quantities by month), a new question may occur to us, such as what the total sales quantities are by sales regions.

Similar R command logic (such as the `barplot` function) can be used to manipulate our data and present this information, as follows:

```
# --- load our data into a data frame object
data.df<-data.frame(x)
# --- initialize some counters one for each sales region ID
R1<-0
R2<-0
R3<-0
R4<-0
R5<-0
# --- loop through the data and accumulate sale quantities
# --- for each sales region
for(i in 1:nrow(data.df))
{
    MonthInData <-data.df[i,6]
if (MonthInData == '1') {R1 <- R1 + data.df[i,3]}
if (MonthInData == '2') {R2 <- R2 + data.df[i,3]}
if (MonthInData == '3') {R3 <- R3 + data.df[i,3]}
if (MonthInData == '4') {R4 <- R4 + data.df[i,3]}
if (MonthInData == '5') {R5 <- R5 + data.df[i,3]}
}
# --- generate our barplot from accumulated data
# --- in R1 through R5
barplot(c(R1, R2, R3, R4, R5), main="Sales Qty by Region", border = "dark
blue", legend.text = c("1","2","3", "4", "5"), col = c("lightblue",
"mistyrose","lightcyan", "Green", "grey"))
```

The generated visualization is as follows:

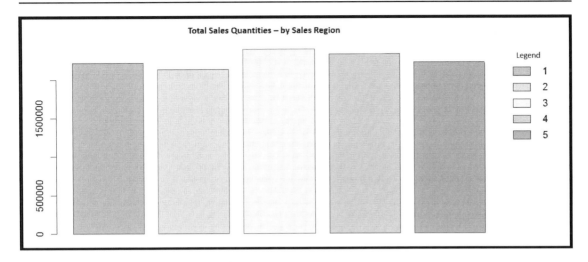

From the previous visualization, of course, further questions can be asked and visualized:

- What is the breakdown of quantities by sales region by month or by quarter?
- What are the quantity totals by product?
- What is the total quantity returned by month, quarter, product, and so on?
- And on and on!

Another way to describe establishing the nature of your data is adding context to it or profiling it. In any case, the objective is to allow the data consumer to better understand the data through visualization.

Another motive for adding context or establishing the nature of your data can be to gain a new perspective on the data. An example of this can be adding comparisons, such as our preceding `sales type` example.

Successful statistical analysis

It is worthwhile to mention some key points in this section, dealing with ensuring a successful (or at least productive) statistical analysis effort.

 You may find that most of these are perhaps common sense notions, but some may not be.

1. As soon as you can, decide on your goal or objective. You need to know what the win is, that is, what the problem or idea is that is driving the analysis effort. In addition, you need to make sure that, whatever is driving the analysis, the result obtained must be measurable in some way. This metric or performance indicator must be identified early.

2. Identify key levers. This means that once you have established your goals and a way to measure performance towards obtaining those goals, you also need to find out what has an effect on the performance towards obtaining each goal.

3. Conduct a thorough data collection. Typically, the more data the better, but in the absence of quantity, always go with quality.

4. Clean your data. Make sure your data has been cleaned in a consistent way so that data issues would not impact your conclusions.

5. Model, model, and model your data. As we mentioned in a prior section, modeling drives modeling. The more you model your data, the more questions you'll have asked and answered, and the better results you'll have.

6. Take time to grow in your statistical analysis skills. It's always a good idea to continue to evolve your experiences and style of statistical analysis. The way to improve is to do it. Another approach is to remodel the data you may have on hand for other projects to hone your skills.

7. Optimize and repeat. As always, you need to take the time for standardizing, following proven practices, using templates, and testing and documenting your scripts and models, so that you can re-use your best efforts over and over again. You will find that this time will be well spent and even your better efforts will improve with use. Finally, share your work with others! The more eyes, the better the product.

Some interesting advice on ensuring success with statistical projects includes the following quote:

> *It's a good idea to build a team that allows those with an advanced degree in statistics to focus on data modeling and predictions, while others in the team-qualified infrastructure engineers, software developers and ETL experts-build the necessary data collection infrastructure, data pipeline and data products that enable streaming the data through the models and displaying the results to the business in the form of reports and dashboards.*
>
> *- G Shapira, 2017*

R and statistical analysis

Just a note here on the use of R for statistical analysis, data profiling exercises as well as adding perspectives (establish context) to data to be used in visualizations.

R is a language and environment that is easy to learn, very flexible in nature, and also very focused on statistical computing, making it great for manipulating, cleaning, summarizing, producing probability statistics (as well as, actually creating visualizations with your data), so it's a great choice for the exercises required for profiling, establishing context, and identifying additional perspectives.

In addition, here are a few more reasons to use R when performing any kind of data or statistical analysis:

- R is used by a large number of academic statisticians, so it's a tool that is not going away.
- R is pretty much platform independent; what you develop will run almost anywhere.
- R has awesome help resources. Just Google it and you'll see!

Summary

In this chapter, we explored the purpose and process of statistical analysis in detail (the differences in data analysis), created a summarization model, and listed the steps involved in a successful statistical analysis. Finally, we underscored the choice of using R as the statistical analysis tool of choice.

The next chapter will be targeted at explaining statistical regression and why it is important to data science. We will walk through the use of various statistical regression methods in everyday data projects and outline how a developer might use regression for simple forecasting and prediction within a typical data development project.

6

Database Progression to Database Regression

In this chapter, we get started by offering a definition for (data) statistical regression, then move on to discussing regression concepts, and outlining how a developer might use the most common regression techniques for forecasting and prediction within a typical data development project.

In this chapter, we've organized information into the following areas:

- An introduction to statistical regression
- Methods for identification of opportunities for using regression (in data projects)
- R and statistical regression
- A working example

Introducing statistical regression

As promised, let's get going in this chapter with a section that provides a clear explanation of what statistical regression is.

For starters, statistical regression is also routinely referred to as regression analysis and is a process for estimating the relationships among variables. This process encompasses numerous techniques for modeling and analyzing variables, focusing on the relationship between a dependent variable and one (or more) independent variables (or **predictors).**

So specifically, regression analysis is the work done to identify and understand how the (best representative) value of a dependent variable (a variable that **depends** on other factors) changes when any one of the independent variables (a variable that **stands alone** and isn't changed by the other variables) is changed while the other independent variables stay the same.

A simple example might be how the total dollars spent on marketing (an independent variable example) impacts the total sales dollars (a dependent variable example) over a period of time (is it really as simple as more marketing equates to higher sales?), or perhaps there is a correlation between the total marketing dollars spent (independent variable), discounting a products price (another independent variable), and the amount of sales (a dependent variable)?

Keep in mind this key point that regression analysis is used to understand which among the independent variables are related to the dependent variable(s), not just the relationship of these variables. Also, the inference of causal relationships (between the independent and dependent variables) is an important objective. However, this can lead to illusions or false relationships, so caution is recommended!

Overall, regression analysis can be thought of as estimating the conditional expectations of the value of the dependent variable, given the independent variables being observed, that is, endeavoring to predict the average value of the dependent variable when the independent variables are set to certain values. I call this the lever affect—meaning when one increases or decreases a value of one component, it directly affects the value at least one other (variable).

An alternate objective of the process of regression analysis is the establishment of location parameters or the quantile of a distribution. In other words, this idea is to determine values that may be a cutoff, dividing a range of a probability distribution values.

You'll find that regression analysis can be a great tool for prediction and forecasting (not just complex machine learning applications). We'll explore some real-world examples later, but for now, let's us look at some techniques for the process.

Techniques and approaches for regression

You'll find that various techniques for carrying out regression analysis have been developed and accepted.

Some research may show the top techniques as the following:

- Linear
- Logistic
- Polynomial
- Stepwise
- Ridge
- Lasso

Here are a quick few words on each:

- **Linear regression**: Linear regression is the most basic type of regression and is commonly used for predictive analysis projects. In fact, when you are working with a single predictor (variable), we call it simple linear regression, and if there are multiple predictor variables, we call it multiple linear regression. Simply put, linear regression uses linear predictor functions whose values are estimated from the data in the model.
- **Logistic regression**: Logistic regression is a regression model where the dependent variable is a categorical variable. This means that the variable only has two possible values, for example, pass/fail, win/lose, alive/dead, or healthy/sick. If the dependent variable has more than two possible values, one can use various modified logistic regression techniques, such as multinomial logistic regression, ordinal logistic regression, and so on.
- **Polynomial regression**: When we speak of polynomial regression, the focus of this technique is on modeling the relationship between the independent variable and the dependent variable as an nth degree polynomial.
    - Polynomial regression is considered to be a special case of multiple linear regressions. The predictors resulting from the polynomial expansion of the baseline predictors are known as **interactive features**.
- **Stepwise regression**: Stepwise regression is a technique that uses some kind of automated procedure to continually execute a step of logic, that is, during each step, a variable is considered for addition to or subtraction from the set of independent variables based on some prespecified criterion.

- **Ridge regression**: Often predictor variables are identified as being interrelated. When this occurs, the regression coefficient of any one variable depends on which other predictor variables are included in the model and which ones are left out. Ridge regression is a technique where a small bias factor is added to the selected variables in order to improve this situation. Therefore, ridge regression is actually considered a remedial measure to alleviate multicollinearity amongst predictor variables.
- **Lasso regression**: Lasso (**least absolute shrinkage selector operator**) regression is a technique where both predictor variable selection and regularization are performed in order to improve the prediction accuracy and interpretability of the result it produces.

Choosing your technique

In addition to the aforementioned regression techniques, there are numerous others to consider with, most likely, more to come. With so many options, it's important to choose the technique that is right for your data and your project.

Rather than selecting the right regression approach, it is more about selecting the most effective regression approach.

Typically, you use the data to identify the regression approach you'll use. You start by establishing statistics or a profile for your data. With this effort, you need to identify and understand the importance of the different variables, their relationships, coefficient signs, and their effect.

Overall, here's some generally good advice for choosing the right regression approach from your project:

1. Copy what others have done and had success with. Do the research. Incorporate the results of other projects into yours. Don't reinvent the wheel. Also, even if an observed approach doesn't quite fit as it was used, perhaps some simple adjustments would make it a good choice.
2. Keep your approach as simple as possible. Many studies show that simpler models generally produce better predictions. Start simple, and only make the model more complex as needed. The more complex you make your model, the more likely it is that you are tailoring the model to your dataset specifically, and generalizability suffers.

3. Check your work. As you evaluate methods, check the residual plots (more on this in the next section of this chapter) because they can help you avoid inadequate models and adjust your model for better results.

4. Use your subject matter expertise. No statistical method can understand the underlying process or subject area the way you do. Your knowledge is a crucial part and, most likely, the most reliable way of determining the best regression approach for your project.

Does it fit?

After selecting a model that you feel is appropriate for use with your data (also known as determining that the approach is the best fit), you need to validate your selection, that is, determine its fit.

A well-fitting regression model results in predicted values close to the observed data values.

The mean model (which uses the mean for every predicted value) would generally be used if there were no informative predictor variables. The fit of a proposed regression model should, therefore, be better than the fit of the mean model.

As a data scientist, you will need to scrutinize the coefficients of determination, measure the standard error of estimate, analyze the significance of regression parameters and confidence intervals (will talk more about these later in this chapter).

Remember that the better the fit of a regression model, most likely the better the precision in, or just better, the results.

It has been proven that simple models produce more accurate results! Keep this always in mind when selecting an approach or technique, and even when the problem might be complex, it is not always obligatory to adopt a complex regression approach.

Identifying opportunities for statistical regression

Typical statistical analysis efforts which often become official statistical projects, start out with determining an objective and then, ultimately, determining the right approach to meet that objective.

Popular data science opinion declares determining an objective as establishing the purpose of a statistical analysis effort, then splits the purpose into three areas:

1. Summarizing data (also called building a data profile)
2. Exposing and exploring relationships between variables in the data
3. Testing the significance of differences (between variables or groups within the data)

Summarizing data

If your statistical objective is to summarize data, you generate descriptive statistics, such as mean, standard deviation, variances, and so on.

Exploring relationships

If your statistical objective is to look for and learn about relationships in your data, you first examine your data for a form or, in other words, ask the question: does your data revolve around frequencies or measurements? From there, the number of predictor variables will dictate to you what regression (or other) approach you should use in your project.

Testing significance of differences

If your statistical objective involves testing the differences (between groups) found in the data, then you start out by identifying both the groups as well as the number of those groups. Data analysis involve data with a single group (of interest) leverages (compares values to) a mean, while data with more than one group can use the number of groups to determine which predictive approach one should consider.

Project profitability

As a real-world example, let's consider a consulting services organization that has data collected describing its project work over time. This organization may be contracted to lead technology and/or business-related projects of all sizes and effort levels. Each project has expenses and revenues. Some projects are profitable, and some are not. The firm is interested in identifying which variables (if any) are candidates for predicting how profitable a project will be, in other words, which variables (in particular) are significant predictors of the dependent variable (in this case profitability)?

Examining the data, we see a good list of both variables and measurements; some of which are listed as follows:

- Number of consultants assigned to the project **full time (FT)**
- Number of consultants assigned to the project **part-time (PT)**
- Number of sub-contractors assigned to the project (FT or PT)
- Number of customer resources assigned to the project full time
- Number of customer resources assigned to the project part-time
- Years of experience with the projects core technology
- Total project management hours
- Total development hours
- Hourly bill rate
- Total hours invoiced
- Number of technologies used in the project
- Project style (Time and materials, not to exceed or staff augment) and so on

Generally while speaking, when the data scientist uses regression analysis, he or she is hoping to answer the following three questions:

1. Does a set of predictor variables do a good job in predicting an outcome variable? In our project profitability example, would the number of full-time consultants assigned to a project do a good job of predicting profitability?
2. Which variables (in particular) are significant predictors of the dependent variable? Again, in our project profitability example, can we identify a significant predictor as the number of full-time consultants assigned to the project or perhaps the total project management hours?

3. What is the regression equation (the estimated relationship or effect of some variables on others) that shows how the set of predictor variables can be used to predict the outcome? In our project profitability example, would the regression equation be this?

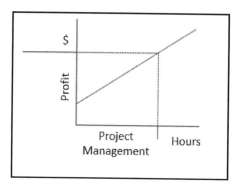

Our project profitability example looks like it could be a reasonable candidate for regression analysis.

In this chapter's next sections, we'll attempt to establish a profile for the project data and then use an appropriate regression technique to establish it. Then, examine variable relationships and, hopefully, predict project profitability based upon selected predictor variables.

R and statistical regression

Before we jump right into our modeling, let's take a moment to validate the use of R as our statistical modeling tool.

R is an open-source statistical environment and a powerful programming language that continues to be one of the most popular choices for statistical modeling. Modeled after S and S-Plus, R has an ever-growing, widespread audience as is well maintained by the R core-development team (an international team of volunteer developers).

R and many related resources can easily be found online along with detailed directions for downloading the software, accompanying packages and other sources of documentation. In addition, there are a ton of specialized routines that have been written for R by people all over the world and made freely available as R packages.

Since R is a programming language, it brings the power of programming to your project, but it does require some expertise with the tool. Thankfully, it offers a **graphical user interface (GUI)** to make things easier and allow you to copy and paste from other sources and projects.

A working example

Let's now get back to our real-world example of project profitability!

We know that our consulting service organizations project results data describes the results of all its project work over time. There are 100 projects (or observations) in our data and consists of two variables hours billed and profit. The first variable is self-explanatory: it's the total number of hours billed to the client for that project. The second is a US dollar amount that equates to the revenues collected from the client after subtracting all expenses (for the project).

We know that each project has both expenses and revenue, and some projects are profitable while others are not. In addition, even projects that are profitable vary greatly in their level of profitability. Again, the firm is interested in identifying which variables (if any) are candidates for predicting how profitable a project will be.

Let's get started with our statistical analysis!

Establishing the data profile

Before attempting to use our project results data to build a regression model, one usually attempts to analyze the data, identifying the key variables. Most often, you would create various visualizations with your data (we walk through this next in this section) in an effort to understand the cause-and-effect relationships among variables or groups within the data.

In statistics, these tasks are commonly referred to as performing a graphical analysis and correlation study.

The graphical analysis

In our statistical analysis example, we want to build a simple regression model that we can use to predict project profitability (profit) by establishing a statistically significant linear relationship with hours billed (to a client) (hours billed). Therefore, we can begin our graphical analysis by plotting this data in various ways.

Typically, for each of the independent variables (predictors), the following plots should be drawn to visualize the following behavior:

- **Scatter plot**: This is drawn to visualize the linear relationship between the predictor and the response.
- **Box plot**: This is drawn to spot any outlier observations in the variable. Having outliers in a predictor can drastically affect the predictions as they can easily affect the direction/slope of the line of best fit.
- **Density plot**: This is drawn to see the distribution of the predictor variable. Ideally, a close to a normal distribution (a bell-shaped curve), without being skewed to the left or right is preferred.

Scatter plots can help visualize any linear relationships between the dependent (response) variable and independent (predictor) variables.

 Ideally, if you are observing multiple predictor variables, a scatter plot should be drawn for each one of them against the response.

Following are the simple R commands that use the variables `HoursBilled` and `Profit` from our project results data to create our scatter plot visualization:

```
# --- load our project results data

MyData <- read.csv(file="c:/Worker/HoursBilledProfit.csv", header=TRUE,
sep=",")

# --- build our scatter plot on the relationship between our
# --- variables

scatter.smooth(x=MyData$HoursBilled, y=MyData$Profit, main="Hours Billed
vs. Profit")   # scatterplot
```

The following graph is our generated scatterplot:

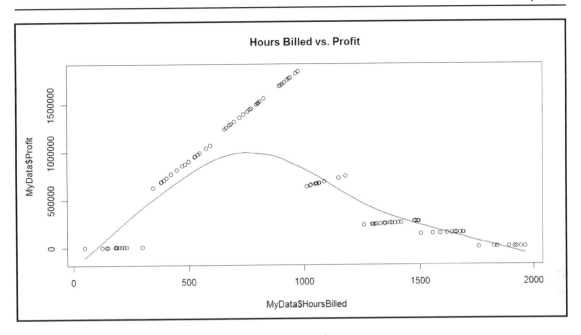

The **Hours Billed vs Profit** scatter plot along with the smoothing line shown in the preceding diagram suggests an initially linearly increasing then decreasing relationship between the total hours billed to a project and the profit variables.

Note that one of the underlying assumptions in linear regression is that the relationship between the response and predictor variables is linear and additive, so this data initially looks like it fits.

Our next step is to look for any outliers in our data. Data points that land outside the 1.5 * interquartile-range (1.5 * IQR) are considered to be outliers, where IQR is calculated as the distance between the 25th percentile and 75th percentile values for that variable.

In a statistical analysis of data, a boxplot is commonly used for graphically depicting groups of numerical data through their quartiles. These visualizations may also have lines extending vertically from the boxes (some data scientists refer to these lines as whiskers), indicating variability outside the upper and lower quartiles. Boxplots are very good for the identification of outliers.

The following R commands are used to some generate boxplots:

```
# --- load our project results data

MyData <- read.csv(file="c:/Worker/HoursBilledProfit.csv", header=TRUE,
```

```
sep=",")

par(mfrow=c(1, 2))    # divide graph area in 2 columns

# --- box plot for hours billed

boxplot(MyData$HoursBilled, main="Hours Billed", sub=paste("Outlier rows:
", boxplot.stats(MyData$HoursBilled)$out))

# --- box plot for Profit

boxplot(MyData$Profit, main="Profit", sub=paste("Outlier rows: ",
boxplot.stats(MyData$Profit)$out))
```

The following are the outlier boxplots for the preceding R commands generated from our project results data:

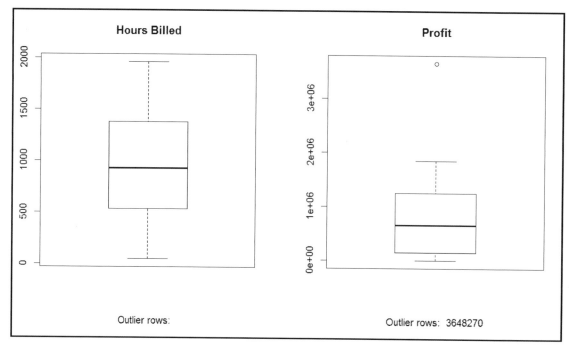

You can notice the outlier identified in the variable profit (on the right side of the preceding figure). The **Outlier rows: 3648270** corresponds to a data point in our file:

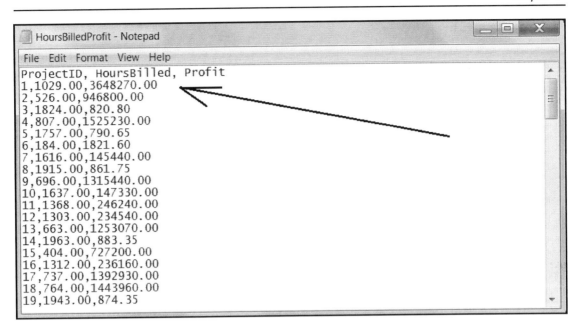

Finally, a density plot can be created to see how close our response variables
(`ProjectID`,`HoursBilled`, and `Profit`) may be to normality. To do this, we can use the
following R commands:

```
# --- load our project results data

MyData <- read.csv(file="c:/Worker/HoursBilledProfit.csv", header=TRUE,
sep=",")
library(e1071)

# --- divide graph area in 2 columns


par(mfrow=c(1, 2))

# --- density plot for profit
plot(density(MyData$Profit), main="Density Plot: Profit", ylab="Frequency",
sub=paste("Skewness:", round(e1071::skewness(MyData$Profit), 2)))
polygon(density(MyData$Profit), col="red")

# --- density plot for hours billed

plot(density(MyData$HoursBilled), main="Density Plot: Hours Billed",
ylab="Frequency", sub=paste("Skewness:",
round(e1071::skewness(MyData$HoursBilled), 2)))
polygon(density(MyData$HoursBilled), col="red")
```

Following are the density plots:

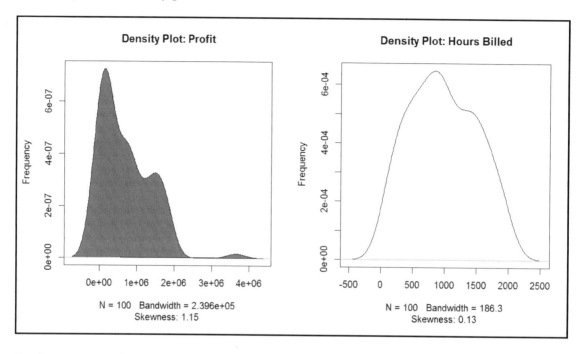

So, do we see a relevant relationship between hoursbilled to a project and how (if at all) profitable the project is?

One way for us to be sure is to establish a correlation between the variables. Correlation suggests the level of linear dependence between two variables that occur in pair, just like what we think we have with hoursbilled and (project) profit.

If the data scientist found that profit increases along with an increase in every project HoursBilled, then there would be a high positive correlation between the two variables, and, therefore, the correlation between them will be closer to 1. Conversely, the opposite is true for an inverse relationship, in which case, the correlation between the variables will be close to -1.

A value closer to 0 suggests a weak relationship between the variables. A low correlation (-0.2 < x < 0.2) probably suggests that much of variation of the response variable (Y) is unexplained by the predictor (X), in which case, we should probably look for better explanatory variables.

The R programming language again provides us with a way to easily accomplish this: the `cor` function, which will determine a correlation between our two variables:

```
> cor(MyData$HoursBilled, MyData$Profit)
[1] -0.2578628
>
```

The given preceding output, we may determine that there really isn't any reason to believe that as the number of hours billed on a projected increase, so does the profitability. Given this information, we should look at some other possible predictor variables.

For the sake of time, (we want to get on with our regression model building) rather than starting over, we'll make an educated guess that perhaps the variable Total project management hours is a good predictor of project profitability. Let's try running the same cor function using this variable:

```
> MyData <- read.csv(file="c:/Worker/ProjectManagementProfit0.csv", header=TRUE, sep=",")
> cor(MyData$ProjectManagement, MyData$Profit)
[1] 0.6138142
>
```

As the preceding calculated correlation indicates (generated again by the use of the R function `cor`), the variable `ProjectManagement` seems to have a higher positive correlation (than hours billed) to project profitability.

Typically, we would take the time to rebuild the visualizations we created earlier in this section using this data (such as the following scatterplot), but again, for the sake of time, we'll move ahead:

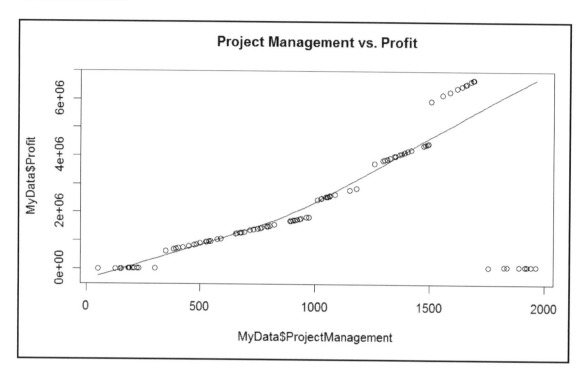

We can see (from our scatterplot: **Profit Management vs. Profit**) that this time, we have a smooth, linear regression of our data in that as the amount of project management time increases, so does the projects overall profitably!

Let's move on!

So now that we have established (what appears to be) a fine linear relationship with visualizations such as a scatter plot (and other examples in the previous section) and then by computing a positive correlation (using the R function `cor`), we can try to construct an actual linear regression model.

Once again, R provides us with a relevant function—lm(). The lm() function takes in two main arguments:

- Formula (an object of class formula)
- Data (typically a data.frame)

Following are the R commands we can use to generate an R regression model:

```
# --- build linear regression model on all of our
# --- project results data

alinearMod <- lm(ProjectManagement ~ Profit, data=MyData)
print(alinearMod)
```

Following are the results of building our model:

```
> # --- build linear regression model on full data
> alinearMod <- lm(ProjectManagement ~ Profit, data=MyData)
> print(alinearMod)

Call:
lm(formula = ProjectManagement ~ Profit, data = MyData)

Coefficients:
(Intercept)        Profit
   6.180          1.629
>
```

Using the preceding R commands to build a linear model, we have established the relationship between the predictor (Project Management hours) and response (the profitability of the project) in the form of a mathematical formula for Project Management (ProjectManagement) as a function of Profit.

We can use the coefficients from the preceding output (Intercept: 6.180 and Profit: 1.629) to create the formula:

$$projectmanagement = -6.180 + 1.629 * profit$$

With our linear model and formula, we can predict the profit value of a project if a corresponding Project Management (total hours) is known. Exciting!

 Although we have established a means for prediction (of project profitability), keep in mind that before using any regression model, you have to ensure that it is statistically significant.

Predicting with our linear model

We just created a linear regression model using R commands with all of our project results data. In the real-world, one would rather chunk the data using what is called the **80:20 sample rule**. This means that 80% of the data will be used for training the model, while the other 20% can be used for testing and validation.

Let's go through this process now.

Step 1: Chunking the data

We can read our project results data in, then use the R sample function to create our 2 two chunks of data (as `trainingData` and `testData`), as shown in the following R commands as follows:

```
# --- first load our project results data
# --- from our CSV file into the object MyData

MyData <- read.csv(file="c:/Worker/ProjectManagementProfit.csv",
header=TRUE, sep=",")

# --- next we are setting the ""sample seed""
# --- to reproduce results of random sampling

set.seed(100)
trainingRowIndex <- sample(1:nrow(MyData), 0.8*nrow(MyData))

# --- create our ""chunk"" of
# --- model training data

trainingData <- MyData [trainingRowIndex,]

# --- create our ""chunk of
# --- test data
testData <- MyData [-trainingRowIndex,]
```

Step 2: Creating the model on the training data

Like we did earlier in this chapter, we can use the R function lm to create our regression model with our trainingData chunk:

```
# --- Build the model on training data

lmMod <- lm(ProjectManagement ~ Profit, data=trainingData)
```

Step 3: Predicting the projected profit on test data

Then, we use the R function predict to create our project predictions, as shown in the following R commands:

```
# --- predict project profitability

ProfitPred <- predict(lmMod, testData)
```

Following is the output generated by the preceding R commands:

```
> # --- predict project profitability
> ProfitPred <- predict(lmMod, testData)
> ProfitPred
         1         3         4         5         7        14        23        29        33        41
 1004.8763  581.3375  833.4984  580.7547 1690.0242  582.5466  747.6671  707.8118  565.5675 1297.7181
        44        59        60        68        69        76        82        88        96       100
 1342.6028  885.3103  565.7636  783.3471 1029.6436 1003.5952  792.6467 1020.2491  804.6033  732.8004
>
```

Step 4: Reviewing the model

Perhaps the final step in our process is to create a summation of the model and review it for statistical significance.

We can use the R function summary:

```
# --- generate the summary of the model

summary (lmMod)
```

This generates the following output:

```
> summary (lmMod)

Call:
lm(formula = ProjectManagement ~ Profit, data = trainingData)

Residuals:
    Min      1Q  Median      3Q     Max
-516.48 -210.30  -43.53   59.69 1360.63

Coefficients:
              Estimate Std. Error t value Pr(>|t|)
(Intercept) 5.655e+02  6.448e+01   8.769 3.03e-13 ***
Profit      1.757e-04  2.136e-05   8.229 3.39e-12 ***
---
Signif. codes:  0 '***' 0.001 '**' 0.01 '*' 0.05 '.' 0.1 ' ' 1

Residual standard error: 383.4 on 78 degrees of freedom
Multiple R-squared:  0.4647,    Adjusted R-squared:  0.4578
F-statistic: 67.71 on 1 and 78 DF,  p-value: 3.393e-12

> |
```

From the preceding output generated, we are shown that our model predictor's p values are visually interpreted as significant, shown by the significance stars at the end of the row (outlined), so we know we have a statistically significant model.

Step 4: Accuracy and error

A simple correlation between the actual values (the actual project profit totals) and the model's predicted (profit) values can be used to test the accuracy of our project profit predictions.

This is illustrated in the following R commands, as follows where we again utilize the R function `cor`:

```
> actuals_preds <- data.frame(cbind(actuals=testData$ProjectManagement, predicteds=distPred))
> correlation_accuracy <- cor(actuals_preds)
> head(actuals_preds)
   actuals predicteds
1     1029  1004.8763
3     1824   581.3375
4      807   833.4984
5     1757   580.7547
7     1616  1690.0242
14    1963   582.5466
> |
```

A high correlation accuracy implies that the actual and predicted values have similar directional movement, that is, when the actual values increase, the predicted also increase, and vice versa; or it is to assume that as the total Project Management hours on a project increase or decrease, the project's profitability increase or decrease in the same manner!

Summary

In this chapter, we introduced a statistical regression, noted the most common regression approaches, and provided some advice on selecting the correction approach for a particular statistical project. In addition, we mentioned how to identify opportunities for using statistical regression and discussed data summarization, exploring relationships, and testing for significance of the difference.

Finally, we wrapped up with a working example of linear regression modeling for r predicting project profitability.

The next chapter will introduce the developer to the idea of statistical regularization for improving data models in an effort to help comprehend what statistical regularization is and why it is important as well as feel comfortable with various statistical regularization methods.

7
Regularization for Database Improvement

In this chapter, we will introduce the idea of statistical regularization to improve data models in an effort to help comprehend what statistical regularization is, why it is important as well as to feel comfortable with the various statistical regularization methods.

In this chapter, we've organized information into the following areas:

- Statistical regularization
- Using data to understand statistical regularization
- Improving data or a data model
- Using R for statistical regularization

Statistical regularization

So, what is statistical regularization?

With regularization, whether we are speaking about mathematics, statistics, or machine learning, we are essentially talking about a process of adding additional information in order to solve a problem.

The term **regularization** has been described as an abstract concept of management of complex systems (according to a set of rules or accepted concepts). These rules will define how one can add or modify values in order to satisfy a requirement or solve a problem.

Does adding or modifying values mean changing data? (More about this will be studied later in this chapter.)

Various statistical regularization methods

Within the statistical community, the most popular statistical regularization methods may include the following:

- Ridge
- Lasso
- Least angles

Ridge

Ridge regression is a statistical technique that is used when analyzing regression data or models that suffer from a condition known as **multicollinearity**. When multicollinearity occurs, estimates may be unbiased but their variances are usually large and far from the true value. This technique adds a degree of bias to the regression estimates to reduce standard errors (to produce estimates that are more dependable).

 Multicollinearity is a condition within statistics in which a predictor (variable) in multiple regression models can be linearly predicted from the others with a significant accuracy.

Lasso

Least absolute shrinkage and selection operator (**Lasso**) is a statistical technique that performs both variable selection and regularization in an effort to enhance prediction accuracies within a model.

 The process of choosing or selecting variables within a statistical model results, obviously, in reducing the number of variables, which is also referred to as variable shrinkage.

Least angles

Least Angle Regression (**LARS**) is a statistical technique used by data scientists when dealing with high-dimensional data. If there is speculation that a response variable is determined by a particular subset of predictors, then the LARS technique can help with determining which variables to include in the regression process.

Opportunities for regularization

So, when would you, a data scientist, consider using any type of regularization method?

Well, the truth is that there is no absolute rule that dictates the use of regularization; however, there are certain indicators to observe that should cause you to consider regularization, for example:

- If your data contains a high variable count
- If there is a low ratio of the number of observations to the number of variables in your data

In `Chapter 6`, *Database Progression to Database Regression* (on statistical regression), we reviewed some sample data consisting of consulting project results. In that example, we explored the relationship between the total hours billed to the project, the total project management hours spent on the project, and the project's supposed profitability.

Looking closer at that same data, perhaps we may now see additional variables, such as the following:

- Number of consultants assigned to the project full time
- Number of consultants assigned to the project part-time
- Number of sub-contractors assigned to the project (full time or part time)
- Number of customer resources assigned to the project full time
- Number of customer resources assigned to the project part-time
- Number of local resources assigned to the project
- Years of experience with the projects core technology
- Total project management hours
- Total development hours
- Hourly bill rate

- Total hours invoiced
- Number of technologies used in the project
- Project style (time and materials, not to exceed, or staff augment)

Here, we can see more than twelve possible independent or predictor variables—certainly a manageable number—especially given that the number of observations (records) in the file is over 100 (the ratio of variables to observations is about 12%).

An independent variable (or experimental or predictor variable) is a variable that is being manipulated in a model to observe the effect on a dependent variable, or an outcome variable.

When a data scientist speaks of high variable counts, they are really referring to an excessive number or, if the number of variables is approaching the number of observations, (not so in this example) but suppose we had more than 50 possible predictor variables in our data of only 100 observations? This is what can be referred to as an overly complex model and warrants consideration of using a common regulation method.

What constitutes as overly complex is often a subject for debate and often differs based on the data and objectives of the statistical model.

Experience shows us that when a model is excessively complex, a model may fit but have a poor predicting performance (which is ultimately the goal). When this occurs, a data scientist will recognize overfitting.

Regularization is the statistical technique used by data scientists to avoid or address this overfitting problem. The idea behind regularization is that models that overfit the data are complex statistical models that have, for example, too many parameters.

Other known opportunities for the use of regulation include the following:

- Instances involving high collinearity
- When a project objective is a sparse solution
- Accounting for variables grouping in high-dimensional data
- Classification

Collinearity

The term **collinearity** describes a statistical situation when a selected predictor variable can be linearly predicted from the others with a considerable degree of accuracy.

 Linear prediction is a procedure where future values of a variable are estimated based on a linear function of previous samples.

This typically allows very small changes to the data to produce unreliable results regarding individual predictor variables. That is, multiple regression models with collinear predictors can indicate how well the entire bundle of predictors predicts the outcome variable, but it may not give valid results about any individual predictor, or about which predictors are redundant with respect to others.

Sparse solutions

A **sparse solution** or **approximation** is a sparse vector that approximately solves an arrangement of equations. Techniques to find sparse approximations have found a wide use in applications such as image processing and document analysis.

 You should recall that a vector is a sequence of data points of the same basic type. Members of a vector are officially called **components**.

High-dimensional data

High-dimensional statistics is the study of data where the number of dimensions is higher than the dimensions considered in the classical **multivariate analysis** (**MVA**).

 In statistical studies, a **multivariate random variable** (or **random vector**) is a list of variables, each of whose value is unknown. MVA is defined as the study of this occasion.

High-dimensional statistics relies on the theory of random vectors. In many applications, the dimension of the data vectors may be larger than the sample size.

Classification

Classification is the process of identifying to which of a set of categories or groups a new observation belongs, on the basis of a training set of data containing observations (or instances) whose category membership is known.

Regularization is a common statistical technique used to address the mentioned (as well as other) scenarios. In the next section, we'll look at some simple examples of each of these.

Using data to understand statistical regularization

Variable selection is an imperative process within the field of statistics as it tries to make models simpler to understand, easier to train, and free of misassociations--by eliminating variables unrelated to the output.

This (variable selection) is one possible approach to dealing with the problem of overfitting. In general, we don't expect a model to completely fit our data; in fact, the problem of overfitting often means that it may be disadvantageous to our predictive model's accuracy on unseen data if we fit our training or test data too well.

Rather than using variable selection, the process of regularization is an alternative approach to reducing the number of variables in the data in order to deal with the issue of overfitting and is essentially a process of introducing an intentional bias or constraint in a training of a model that (hopefully) prevents our coefficients from exhibiting very high variances.

When the number of parameters (in a population) is deemed very large—particularly compared to the number of available observations—linear regression tends to allow small changes in a few of the observations to cause the coefficients to change drastically (or, as we already put it, exhibit very high variances).

Ridge regression is a statistical method that introduces a controlled bias (through or using a constraint) to the model's regression estimates but is effective at reducing the model's variance as well.

 Ridge regression is sometimes referred to within the data scientist community as a penalized regression technique.

There are a number of different R functions and packages that implement ridge regression, such as `lm.ridge()` from the MASS package and `ridge()` from the genridge package.

 You might be familiar with the MASS R package but perhaps not genridge. The genridge package introduces generalizations of the standard univariate ridge trace plot used in ridge regression and related methods and is worthy of additional investigation.

In Chapter 6, *Database Progression to Database Regression* we proposed an example where we created a linear regression model on data from a consulting company's project results in an effort to predict a project's profitability. We used the R function: `lm()`, which takes in two main arguments: `formula` (an object of class formula) and `data` (typically a `data.frame`), as shown in the following R code:

```
# --- build linear regression model using all the
# --- project results data
alinearMod <- lm(ProjectManagement ~ Profit, data=MyData)
```

In this chapter, we are going to work with the `lm.ridge()` function in an attempt to acceptably fit the preceding linear model using ridge regression. The preceding code generated a linear model using our R object named `MyData`, using the `ProjectManagment` variable to predict `Profit`.

The `lm.ridge` function uses the following syntax:

```
lm.ridge(formula, data, subset, na.action, lambda = 0, model = FALSE,
x = FALSE, y = FALSE, contrasts = NULL, ...)
```

The arguments are included here for later reference:

- `formula`: This a formula expression as for regression models, of the form response ~ predictors
- `data`: This is an optional data frame in which to interpret the variables occurring in the formula
- `subset`: This is an expression saying which subset of the rows of the data should be used in the fit. All observations are included by default
- `na.action`: This a function to filter missing data
- `lambda`: This is a scalar or vector of ridge constants
- `model`: Should the model frame be returned?
- `x`: Should the design matrix be returned?

- y: Should the response be returned?
- contrasts: A list of contrasts to be used for some or all of the factor terms in the formula

 The term lambda (here, a parameter in the lm.ridge function) is typically defined as a comparison of a group means on a combination of dependent variables.

To set up our next example, let's recall that our project data had a ratio of variables to observations of 12%. Suppose we've been provided with a new data file, one which has only 50 observations. Now our ratio of variables to observations goes up to 24%.

What about a file with only 12 observations? Further, suppose we are told that management believes that these 12 observations are based upon the key, high-visibility projects and therefore are unwilling to provide a bigger population to the data scientist (at least at this time)? Is it even worthwhile to model this data? Would the results be valuable in any way?

In general terms, it is said that the more the variables present in a regression model, the more flexible a model is considered to be, or that it will become. It is very likely that a model of this type will be able to achieve a low error by fitting random fluctuations in the training data but the outcome or results won't represent the true, underlying distribution of the variables within the data and in other words, performance will, therefore, be poor when the model is run on future data drawn from the same distribution. (Management would not be happy if our predictions for project profitability were based upon flawed logic!)

Given the preceding scenario, how should a data scientist proceed? Well, it is certainly possible to fit good models when there are more variables than data points, but it must be done very carefully.

As a rule, when the data contains more variables than observations, the results may seemingly yield acceptable performance, but as we already mentioned, the solution may achieve favorable results or even zero error on the training data. Such a model would certainly overfit on actual data because it's too flexible for the amount of training data. (This condition is called **ill-posed** or **underdetermined**.)

This problem is most often addressed by carefully setting limitations or imposing constraints on the parameters, either explicitly or via a logical process. The model then becomes a trade-off between fitting the data well and satisfying these set limits or constraints. Ridge regression constraints or penalizes data parameters and can yield better predictive performance by limiting the model's flexibility, thereby reducing the tendency to overfit.

However, simply setting limits or imposing constraints doesn't imply that the resulting solution will be good or acceptable. Constraints will only produce good solutions when they're actually suited to the problem or objective at hand.

Let's get back to the `lm.ridge` function we mentioned earlier in the section. A little different from the use of the `lm` function, we can see the difference in the following use case examples.

Typical to most examples you'll find, we can utilize the `runif` and `rnom` R functions to generate some random number datasets (to be used for illustration), we can see the difference between executing `lm` and `lm.ridge`:

```
# -- create a uniform random number series as X1, X2 and X3
# --- using runif
x1 <- runif(n=20)
x2 <- runif(n=20)
x3 <- runif(n=20)
# --- Create a new variable from x1 and x2
x3c <- 10*x1 + x3
# --- create a random number
ep <- rnorm(n=20)
y <- x1 + x2 + ep
```

As we know what we want to explore (for example, estimating the parameters in a linear regression model), we can take liberties with creating the testing data. The following is an example of R code that generates a linear regression model using our three made-up variables:

```
# --- using the R lm function to create an ordinary least squares (OLS) # -
- fit of 3-variable model using x3 as an independent x3 variable
ols <- lm(y~ x1 + x2 + x3)
summary(ols)
```

The following is the generated output from the preceding code:

```
> ols <- lm(y~ x1 + x2 + x3)
> summary(ols)

Call:
lm(formula = y ~ x1 + x2 + x3)

Residuals:
     Min      1Q   Median      3Q      Max
-1.19698 -0.28592  0.04026  0.24016  1.20322

Coefficients:
            Estimate Std. Error t value Pr(>|t|)
(Intercept)  -0.4293     0.4916  -0.873   0.3954
x1            1.7851     0.4812   3.710   0.0019 **
x2            0.7119     0.4622   1.540   0.1430
x3            0.2839     0.5122   0.554   0.5870
---
Signif. codes:  0 '***' 0.001 '**' 0.01 '*' 0.05 '.' 0.1 ' ' 1

Residual standard error: 0.6306 on 16 degrees of freedom
Multiple R-squared:  0.4831,    Adjusted R-squared:  0.3862
F-statistic: 4.984 on 3 and 16 DF,   p-value: 0.0125

> |
```

Now, let's move on.

Using our same made-up example data and similar thinking, we can use the R function `lm.ridge` to attempt to fit our linear model using ridge regression:

```
# --- Fit model using ridge regression using independent variables
ridge <- lm.ridge (y ~ x1 + x2 + x3, lambda = seq(0, .1, .001))
summary(ridge)
```

The following is the output generated (note the difference in output generated by the `summary` function):

```
> # --- Fit model using ridge regression using independent variables
>
> ridge <- lm.ridge (y ~ x1 + x2 + x3, lambda = seq(0, .1, .001))
> summary(ridge)
       Length Class  Mode
coef   303    -none- numeric
scales   3    -none- numeric
Inter    1    -none- numeric
lambda 101    -none- numeric
ym       1    -none- numeric
xm       3    -none- numeric
GCV    101    -none- numeric
kHKB     1    -none- numeric
kLW      1    -none- numeric
> |
```

You'll find that the `summary` function does not yield the same output on a linear regression model as it does on a model using the ridge regression method. However, there are a variety of packages available to produce sufficient output on ridge regression models.

Improving data or a data model

There are various parameters which are used for improving data or data model. In this section, we will be studying about a few of them.

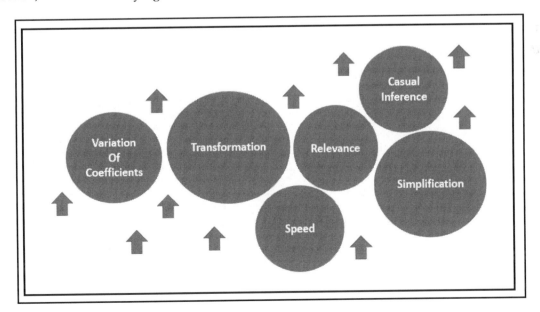

There are much other acceptable or at least well-known methods or approaches that a data scientist may employ in an attempt to improve on a statistical model (other than regularization) and it's worth spending some time mentioning a few of the most popular:

- Simplification
- Relevance
- Speed
- Transformation
- Variation of coefficients
- Casual inference
- Back to regularization
- Reliability

Simplification

The first may be just plain common sense. A simple model is just plain easier to interpret and understand. Algorithms run more efficiently on a simpler model, allowing the data scientist the luxury of higher iterations as well as more time to evaluate the outcomes.

Keep in mind, though, that a more complicated model is somewhat more believable, so beware of over-simplification. The approach to finding the right mix between complex and simple can be worked both ways; by starting simple and adding complexities or, more commonly, by starting complex and removing things out of the model, testing, and evaluating and then repeating, until successfully understanding the (fitting) process.

Relevance

This one also seems obvious as well. In other words, don't waste time on statistical noise. Using common statistical regression packages, you will have visuals (such as quantile-quantile plots, influence diagrams, box plots, and so on) to pour over and understand. Spending time on removing irrelevancies from a model or data will pay dividends. The trick is to be able to identify what is relevant.

Speed

The faster a data scientist can fit models, the more models (and data) can be evaluated and understood (the ultimate goal!). The ways and means of model optimization can be costly-- either in time or expertise--and can focus on the model or the data, or both.

Transformation

This is something that can have a substantial effect on a model, but is not without risk. Transformation of variables can create models that could make sense (and can then be fit and compared to data) and that includes all relevant information, but if done irrationally, may introduce bias and imply incorrect outcomes.

Variation of coefficients

Testing coefficients to determine whether a coefficient should vary by group, and the estimated scale of variation, is a feasible approach to model improvement. Very small varying coefficients (across categories) have the propensity to be dropped out of consideration.

Casual inference

You may be tempted to set up a single large regression to answer several causal questions that exist in a model or data; however, in observational settings (including experiments in which certain conditions of interest are observational), this approach risks bias. The bottom line here is, don't assume anything about any perceived relationships (or coefficients), especially don't assume that a coefficient can be interpreted causally. However, a casual inference can be effective (where appropriate) as a method used to improve a statistical model.

Back to regularization

Getting to the point--the theme of regularization is an attempt to improve an outcome or performance of a statistical model or method. In other words, to improve the process of learning (from data of course) through direct and indirect observation.

The process of attempting to gain knowledge or learn from a finite dataset (also known as **empirical learning**) is said to be an **underdetermined problem**, because in general, it is an attempt to infer a function x $\{\displaystyle\ x\}$, given only some examples of data observations.

Another possible method of improving a statistical model is to use **additive smoothing** (also known as **Laplacian smoothing**) during the training of a model. This is a form of regularization and it works by adding a fixed number to all the counts of feature and class combinations during model training.

 It is a popular opinion that additive smoothing is more effective than other probability smoothing methods in several retrieval tasks such as language model-based applications.

Regularization fundamentally works to introduce additional information, or an intentional bias, or constraint in a training procedure—preventing coefficients from taking large values—in order to solve an ill-posed problem. This is a method that attempts to shrink coefficients, also known as a **shrinkage method**. The information introduced tends to be in the form of a penalty for complexity, such as restrictions for smoothness or bounds on the vector space norm. In other words, regularization A does what it implies, it regulates how or how much you can change a parameter within a statistical model or its data. Yes, that is right, you can change the actual data!

When is it justifiable to change the values of your data?

The statistical community respects that the theoretical justification for regularization might be that it attempts to impose the belief that among competing hypotheses, the one with the fewest assumptions will be the most effective (and therefore should be the one selected and used). This belief is rigorously known as **Occam's razor** (or the law of parsimony).

Reliability

Should one always (Of course, we are referring to those situations that are identified as we discussed in this chapter's section, *Opportunities for regulation*.) attempt to institute a regulation method on a statistical model? Will it always improve a model or data population?

Before considering an answer to this question, remember that regularization does not improve the performance on the dataset that the algorithm initially used to learn the model parameters (feature weights). However, it can improve the generalization performance (the performance on new, unseen data, which is what you are looking for).

Think of using regularization in a statistical model as the adding of bias as a countermeasure to overfitting; on the other hand, though, adding too much bias almost always results in underfitting and the model will perform badly.

Answer: Regularization doesn't always work and may cause a model to perform poorly (perhaps even worse than before!). S. Raschka, Author of Python Machine Learning, makes an interesting comment:

> *In intuitive terms, you can think of regularization as a penalty against the complexity (of a model). Increasing the regularization strength penalizes large weight coefficients. Therefore, your goal is to prevent your model from picking up peculiarities or noise and to generalize well to new, unseen data.*

Using R for statistical regularization

There are a number of different functions and packages that implement ridge regression, such as `lm.ridge()` from the MASS package and `ridge()` from the `genridge` package. For the lasso, there is also the `lars` package. Here, in this chapter, we are going to use R's `glmnet()` function (from the `glmnet` package) due to it being well-documented and having a consistent and friendly interface.

The key to working with regularization is to determine an appropriate `lambda` value to use. The approach that the `glmnet()` function uses is to use a grid of different `lambda` values, training a regression model for each value. Then, one can either pick a value manually or use a technique to estimate the best `lambda`.

You can specify the sequence of the values to try (via the `lambda` parameter); otherwise, a default sequence with 100 values will be used.

Parameter Setup

The first parameter to the `glmnet()` function must be a matrix of features (which we can create using the R function, `model.matrix()`). The second parameter is a vector with the output variable. Finally, the `alpha` parameter is a switch between ridge regression (0) and lasso (1). The following code sets up for our example:

```
# --- load the package
library(glmnet)
# --- create our parameter data
cars_train_mat <- model.matrix(Price ~ .-Saturn, cars_train)[,-1]
lambdas <- 10 ^ seq(8, -4, length = 250)
```

The `model.matrix` R function creates a matrix by expanding factors to a set of summary variables (depending on the contrasts) and expanding interactions similarly.

```
 # --- create regression model
cars_models_ridge <-
   glmnet(cars_train_mat, cars_train$Price, alpha = 0, lambda = lambdas)

# --- create a lasso model
cars_models_lasso <-
   glmnet(cars_train_mat, cars_train$Price, alpha = 1, lambda = lambdas)
```

The preceding code that we used to set up the data to be used in this example (specifically, `length = 250`) provided a sequence of 250 values. This means that (in the preceding code) actually trained 250 ridge regression models and another 250 lasso models!

We can review the value of the `lambda` attribute (of the `cars_models_ridge` object) that is produced by `glmnet()` and then apply the `coef()` function to this object to retrieve the corresponding coefficients for the 100th model, as follows:

```
# --- print the value of the lambda object of the 100th model
# --- generated by glmnet
cars_models_ridge$lambda[100]
[1] 1694.009
```

```
# --- use coef to see 100th model's coefficient values
coef(cars_models_ridge)[,100]
    (Intercept)         Mileage        Cylinder           Doors
   6217.5498831      -0.1574441    2757.9937160     371.2268405
         Cruise           Sound         Leather           Buick
   1694.6023651     100.2323812    1326.7744321    -358.8397493
       Cadillac           Chevy         Pontiac            Saab
  11160.4861489   -2370.3268837   -2256.7482905    8416.9209564
     convertible       hatchback           sedan
  10576.9050477   -3263.4869674   -2058.0627013
```

Finally, we can use the R `plot()` function to obtain a plot showing how the values of the coefficients change as the logarithm values change.

As shown in the following code, it is very helpful to show the corresponding plot for ridge regression and lasso side by side:

```
# --- visualize our model data
# --- set matrix column-widths and the row-heights
layout(matrix(c(1, 2), 1, 2))
```

```
# --- create ridge regression plot
plot(cars_models_ridge, xvar = "lambda", main = "Ridge
    Regression\n")
```

The following is the plot graphic generated by the preceding R code:

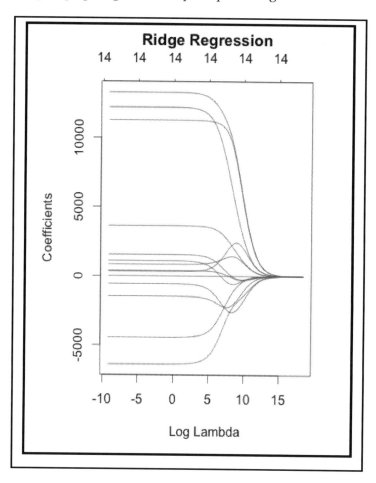

This is the R code to generate the `lasso` plot:

```
# --- create lasso plot
plot(cars_models_lasso, xvar = "lambda", main = "Lasso\n")
```

This is the corresponding output:

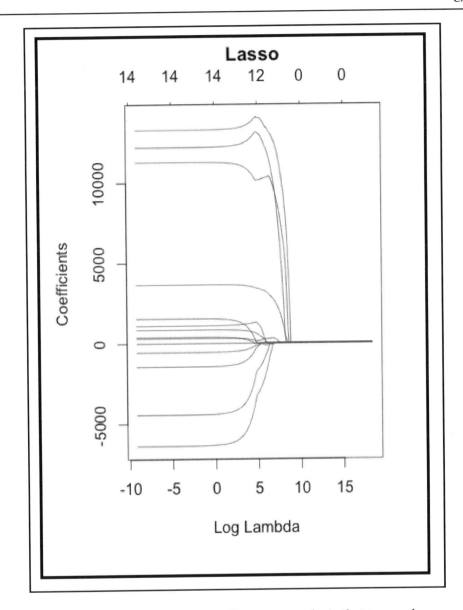

The significant difference between the preceding two graphs is that `lasso` forces many coefficients to fall to zero exactly, whereas, in ridge regression, they tend to drop off smoothly and only become zero altogether at extreme values. Note the values on the top horizontal axis of both of the graphs, which show the number of non-zero coefficients as values vary.

Along with applying regularization to minimize the issue of overfitting, the `lasso` function is often used to perform feature selection as a feature with a zero coefficient would not be included in the model.

As a part of the `glmnet` package, the `predict()` function operates in a variety of contexts. We can, for example, determine the **coefficient variance (CV)** percentages (the strength and direction of a linear relationship between two variables) of a model for a `lambda` value that was not in our original list.

 Predict is a generic function for predictions from the results of various model fitting functions.

Let's try using `predict` on our lasso model (created earlier).

We can write the following R code on our previously created lasso model, `cars_models_lasso`:

```
# --- use predict function on the lasso model
predict(cars_models_lasso, type = "coefficients", s = lambda_lasso)

Below is the generated output, a list of the coefficient values:

 (Intercept)  -521.3516739
Mileage         -0.1861493
Cylinder      3619.3006985
Doors         1400.7484461
Cruise         310.9153455
Sound          340.7585158
Leather        830.7770461
Buick         1139.9522370
Cadillac     13377.3244020
Chevy         -501.7213442
Pontiac      -1327.8094954
Saab         12306.0915679
convertible  11160.6987522
hatchback    -6072.0031626
sedan        -4179.9112364
```

From the preceding output, you can see that `lasso` has not forced any coefficients to zero, in this case, suggesting that none should be removed (and therefore remain as features in the model) from the data.

Summary

In this chapter, we provided an explanation of statistical regularization and then used sample data in an example to illustrate and better understand statistical regularization. Later, we had a discussion of various methods on how to improve (the performance of) data or a data model with regulation. Finally, we saw how well the R language supports the concepts and methods of regulation.

In the next chapter, we're looking to cover the idea of data model assessment and using statistics for assessment. We'll compare the concepts of data assessment and data quality assurance, and finally, apply the idea of statistical assessment to data using R.

8

Database Development and Assessment

In this chapter, we will cover the practice of data (database) assessment. We will provide an understanding of what statistical assessment is, and why it is important to the data scientist, as well as providing instructive examples using R to perform various statistical assessment methods.

As we have been endeavoring to do throughout this book, we will draw similarities between certain data developer and data scientist concepts, looking at the differences between data or database development and data (database) assessment, as well as offer a comparison between the practice of data assessment and data (quality) assurance.

We've organized information in this chapter into the following areas:

- Comparison of assessment and statistical assessments
- Development versus assessment
- Is data assessment an assurance of data quality?
- Applying the idea of statistical assessment to your data using R

Let's get started!

Assessment and statistical assessment

Merriam-Webster defines assessment as:

The action or an instance of making a judgment about something.

The following image shows flow for assessing statistical data:

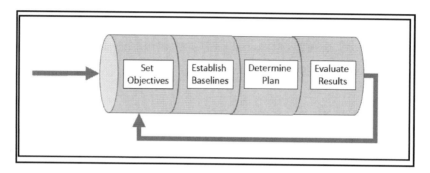

We need to keep a few pointers in mind for statistical assessment. They are listed as follows.

Objectives

With that in mind, to be able to make a reasonable assessment--that is, make a judgment--on something (anything really), one must first have to set objective(s). Assessment objectives help the data scientist determine how to assess data, a database, or a statistical data model. Without clear objectives, you'll waste valuable time, and potentially, put confidence in a model that doesn't meet a business requirement or may even lead to incorrect assumptions (predictions).

Baselines

Next, (based on your set objectives) standards, minimum acceptable performance, or a baseline to establish an opinion on what is being assessed need to be established. In other words, how well does what you are assessing compare to what you agree is acceptable?

Although we won't spend any significant time here on the process of database assessment (rather focus on statistical data or statistical data model assessment), we will mention the use of specific measures of performance (performance measures or metrics).

Data scientists will frequently use very specific (performance) metrics when evaluating the predictive accuracy of a statistical model. These metrics depend on the class or type of the problem being assessed and require one to use slightly different ways of assessing (the model's) performance. This approach also survives as a rule to assess standard, non-statistical data and databases. For example, there are specific performance metrics used to assess an **online transaction processing (OLTP)** data model and those will be quite different from those used to assess an **enterprise data warehouse (EDW)** model.

Looking a little deeper, when evaluating, performance testing, or assessing a (non-statistical) database, one would focus on the identification of various benchmarks (that is, benchmarking), capacity determination and planning, executing soaking or soak tests, peak-rest intervals (to name a few examples) as part of the effort.

Planning for assessment

Just as the type of non-statistical database (OLTP, EDW, and so on) would determine what tests would be used to perform an assessment, so would the type of statistical model (for example, regression, classification, binary classification, and so on) dictate the appropriate assessment techniques or methods (more on this later in this chapter) a data scientist would use to assess a statistical model.

Once you have set the objectives for an assessment and established a baseline, an execution plan is developed. The plan typically outlines the entire process to be performed. The plan will list the tests to be performed along with the test objectives, baselines to be compared to, and even expected outcomes.

Evaluation

In statistics, the term **performance** is usually interchangeably with the idea of a model's accuracy. When speaking about a non-statistical database or model, performance is perhaps all about speed—how long it takes for a query to return values, how long it takes to commit a transaction, and so on—and accuracy, and usually revolves around the idea of quality assurance, not an ability to predict values!

When assessing statistical models, a data scientist will look at a model's error rate, the number of misclassifications (that were made by a model), the ratio of the number of correctly predicted compared to the total number of predicted instances (by the model), and more. Again, all of this is dependent on the statistical model type and the objectives.

Finally, once completed, the results of both a database and statistical data model assessment typically will be visualized in various ways for easier evaluation, using commonly accepted methods (again, how one exposes or visualizes process results will depend on the objectives of the one preparing the visualizations or the objectives of the model). It should be understood that it is not uncommon for various portions of an assessment process (or even the entire assessment process) to be repeated once the results of the assessment have been evaluated. This may be to further clarify something identified in the presented results or for revalidation of certain results. In some situations, new project objectives, baselines, and even a new plan may be developed and executed.

To summarize, the process of performing a database or (statistical) data model assessment is, in a broad sense, similar to that both require the following:

- Set objectives (of the database or data model)
- Establish baselines (to compare performances too)
- Determine (the) plan (to carry out the assessment)
- Evaluate the results

Development versus assessment

Although an assessment process does produce output, which ultimately is perhaps just a decision (that is, does the data, database, or statistical data model under observation meet the acceptable limits of performance, based on the objectives?), development implies building.

Development can also mean improving by expanding, enlarging, or refining. This means that (or at least it implies that) whatever one is developing may never be completely done. In fact, development and assessment do go hand in hand.

An industry-proven practice recommendation to develop anything is as follows:

- Build (or develop)
- Test
- Assess
- Repeat

When developing a relational data model, one might utilize a `create` SQL statement, something like the following code:

```
mysql> CREATE TABLE test (a INT NOT NULL AUTO_INCREMENT,
-> PRIMARY KEY (a), KEY(b))
-> ENGINE=MyISAM SELECT b,c FROM test2;
```

Dissecting the preceding code, we can see that the outcome is that a table object `test` is generated. Perhaps, keeping the same in mind, assessing a (relational) database or data model might use some form of the following code example:

```
USE AdventureWorks;
GO
SET STATISTICS IO ON
SET STATISTICS TIME ON
SELECT p.Name, pr.ProductReviewID
FROM Production.Product p
JOIN Production.ProductReview pr
ON p.ProductID = pr.ProductID
SET STATISTICS IO OFF
SET STATISTICS TIME OFF
```

Statements like the preceding ones execute performance tools that return relevant statistics that can be visualized and analyzed.

A comparable (although simplistic) statistical development (or create) example might look like the following R code (taken from `Chapter 7`, *Regularization for Database Improvement*):

```
# --- using the R lm function to create an ordinary least squares (OLS) # -
- fit of 3-variable model using x3 as an independent x3 variable
ols <- lm(y~ x1 + x2 + x3)
summary(ols)
```

Also from Chapter 7, *Regularization for Database Improvement,* we used the R function summary to start performing some assessment of the performance of the generated linear regression model:

```
> ols <- lm(y~ x1 + x2 + x3)
> summary(ols)

Call:
lm(formula = y ~ x1 + x2 + x3)

Residuals:
     Min       1Q    Median       3Q       Max
-1.19698 -0.28592   0.04026   0.24016   1.20322

Coefficients:
            Estimate Std. Error t value Pr(>|t|)
(Intercept)  -0.4293     0.4916  -0.873   0.3954
x1            1.7851     0.4812   3.710   0.0019 **
x2            0.7119     0.4622   1.540   0.1430
x3            0.2839     0.5122   0.554   0.5870
---
Signif. codes:  0 `***' 0.001 `**' 0.01 `*' 0.05 `.' 0.1 ` ' 1

Residual standard error: 0.6306 on 16 degrees of freedom
Multiple R-squared:  0.4831,    Adjusted R-squared:  0.3862
F-statistic: 4.984 on 3 and 16 DF,  p-value: 0.0125

> |
```

As mentioned earlier, depending on the **class** of a statistical problem, the data scientist will use different approaches or methods to assess (a model's) performance (including the R function summary).

Planning

In the previous section of this chapter, we compared and drew similarities between assessment and statistical assessment and also noted that as part of any assessment project (or at least one that you want to be successful), you need to create a plan.

Moving on to this section where we are relating development and assessment, we again see that the first step in the process of developing is perhaps to create a plan.

 The author believes that the act of creating a plan is a basic requirement for any endeavor in life, even getting up in the morning!

The plan that one creates when having database development in mind can be used as both a guidebook when implementing (in this case, a database or statistical data model) as well as a functional specification (for the database) after implementing it.

What about the task of assessing a database (or in statistics, a data model)? Well, the same applies. The first step is to develop a detailed assessment plan, again that can be used to guide the entire assessment process, then become a functional specification reference after the assessment is completed.

Planning always pays for itself. A good development or assessment plan can become a detailed project plan, an acceptance testing plan, documentation for deployment, and, as already mentioned, a functional specification reference.

Database design is part of the process of data or database development. Designing a database can be a complex task. Part of the design process is for a data modeler (or very experienced data developer) to study the data, its source(s), the requirements, and so on, then produce a detailed data model. This data model will contain all of the needed logical as well as physical design choices as well as the physical storage parameters needed to generate a design in a **data definition language** (**DDL**), which can then be used to actually create the database.

A comprehensive database development plan would include the database design phase (modeling through creation) as well as call-outs to multiple testing and evaluation steps along the way.

Statistical modeling (actually considered to be a form of mathematical modeling) involves embodying or pulling together a set of assumptions concerning or about the generation of some sample data and similar data from a (hopefully) much bigger population (of data).

A plan for the generation of a statistical model would (similar to a plan to generate a database model) include the examination of (sample) data, its source(s), all requirements, and so on. Again, as with the previously mentioned plan, the statistical modeling plan would include mentioning of each assessment and evaluation that the data scientist plans to use on the statistical model.

Typically, a statistical model assessment plan would also include references to the visualizations that the data scientist plans to make the point or summarize the results following each assessment test.

Statistical modeling has been described as studying a system or process to predict its future behavior, as said by Madhuri Kulkarni:

> *With the availability of observed data of a system, models can help infer various alternatives for the system.*

Of all the generic tools that can be used for statistical modeling (and to understand and manipulate data), R seems to be the most powerful and the most popular.

From a non-statistical modeling perspective, data modeling defines and analyzes the requirements to support the business process (within the space of certain information systems in the organization). Here, tools such as Erwin Data Modeler and MySQL Workbench seem to constitute the tools most often successfully used.

Finally, although development and assessment are separate efforts, they are intimately related and, statistical or non-statistical, one does not exist without the existence of the other.

Data assessment and data quality assurance

To be methodical with our discussions here, let's look at how data assessment compares or stacks up to data quality (assurance).

Data quality assurance, or often referred to as **tidying the data** by data scientists, is the process of addressing (perhaps perceived) issues or concerns that had been identified within data. These issues affect the use, quality, and outcome (performance) of a database or data model—data quality, of course, being relative to the proposed purpose of use (of the data, database, or data model).

Categorizing quality

Typically, issues with data quality may be categorized into one of the following areas:

- Accuracy
- Completeness
- Update Status

- Relevance
- Consistency (across sources)
- Reliability
- Appropriateness
- Accessibility

You'll find plenty of data quality categorizing overlap between statistical and non-statistical data. Sometimes, a data quality issue may appear to apply strictly to a particular genre—stat versus non-stat—but after further investigation or at least more experience with the data or in the field, you may find the quality is quality.

The quality of data can affect outcomes and data's quality can be affected by the way it is entered, stored, and managed and the process of addressing data quality (referred to most often as quality assurance, **data quality assurance** (**DQA**)) requires a routine and regular review and evaluation of the data and, performing on-going processes termed profiling and scrubbing. (This is vital even if the data is stored in multiple disparate systems making these processes difficult.)

Although the concept of data quality assurance and tidying data are similar in many ways, DQA is typically much more focused on repeatable processes, while tidying is most often as needed and at the discretion of the data scientist, based on the objectives of the statistical model (although the experienced data scientist would most likely make an effort to create reusable routines or scripts that can be used by them later to manipulate or tidy data on this particular project or others).

Relevance

A lot of noteworthy emphases can be found on statistical relevance. The relevance of statistical information reflects the degree to which it meets the real needs of a particular project. It is concerned with whether the available information sheds light on the concerns that are important to the project. Assessing relevance is subjective and depends on the varying needs of users.

One of the key methods to establish and measure the relevance of data is through a process known as **adding context** or **profiling**.

Let's see, what is this profiling?

Generally speaking, similarly looking data can actually mean very different things. For example, the average **revolutions per minute** (**RPM**) carries a different connotation if the data represents sports cars compared to economy cars or even trucks.

With data, context clues should be developed, through the process we've mentioned referred to as profiling, so that the data consumer can better understand (the data) when used. Additionally, having context and perspective on the data you are working with is a vital step in determining what kind of assessments should be performed or, in the case to a non-statistical model, perhaps the kind of performance evaluations might best suit.

Another motive to add context to data might be to gain a new perspective on the data. An example of this might be recognizing and examining a comparison present in the data. For example, home or housing values could be compared by zip code or other criteria.

Adding context to data (statistical or otherwise) as part of the development and assessment process (recall that we mentioned the two go hand in hand) can certainly make it (the data) more relevant, but context still can't serve as a substitute for value.

Before you consider any variables within your data, such as average rpm, torque, top speed, wheelbase, weight (or whatever), first and foremost, assessment testing needs to benefit those who are going to consume it or, in other words, whatever the data scientist is interested in predicting. For example, if we were to extend this vehicle data example, the expected MPG or miles per gallon, so establishing appropriate context requirements will be critical.

For data profiling (or adding context to the data you will be using in a project), the rule is as follows:

Before Context, Think –> Value

Similar to how we categorized the types of data quality issues, there are several contextual categories, which can be used to argument or increase the value and understanding of data for visualization:

- Definitions and explanations
- Comparisons
- Contrasts
- Tendencies
- Dispersion

Assessment value and data quality, or even data or data model value, although may have areas of overlap, have different objectives.

Cross-validation

We cannot have a chapter in a book focusing on statistics (and assessing statistical models) without a least a section on cross-validation. You may hear some data scientists refer to cross-validation as rotation estimation or simply a general technique to assess models.

Cross-validation is one of the most common methods a data scientist may use to assess how accurately a statistical model will perform. The key concept of cross-validation is testing a model's ability to generalize or, specifically, how well the model applies what it infers from training on data samples (to an entire population or dataset).

 There are two goals in cross-validation—estimating the performance of a model from available data using one algorithm, and comparing the performance of two or more different algorithms and finding out the best algorithm for the available data.

At a high level, the process of cross-validation is to identify a known dataset called the **validation dataset**, train on that dataset, then the second dataset of unknown data (or first seen data) against which the algorithm or data model will be tested (this is known as your **testing dataset**). The objective here is to try to ensure that complications like overfitting (allowing non-inclusive information to influence results) are controlled, as well as to provide some understanding on how the model will generalize a real problem or on a real data file.

Preparing data

To perform cross-validation, the data scientist must prepare the data. This work will consist of gaining an understanding of the data through profiling (which we mentioned in an earlier section of this chapter) so that the data can be separated into samples of comparable subsets. One subset of the data is then determined to be the training set and the analysis is performed on it. Next, once the analysis (or training) is completed, the result (or performance) is validated using the other subset (called the **validation set** or **testing set**).

To reduce variability, multiple iterations (also called **folds** or **rounds**) of cross-validation are performed using different partitions, and the validation results are averaged over the rounds.

Typically, a data scientist will use a model's stability to determine the actual number of rounds of cross-validation that should be performed:

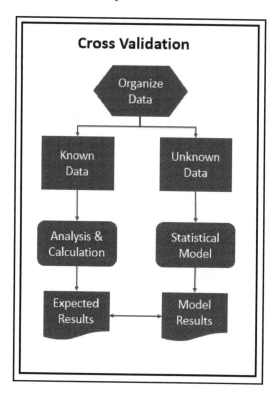

As you can see in the preceding screenshot, the **Cross Validation** method can perhaps be better understood by thinking about the data scientist organizing a population of data into two subsets: **Known Data** and **Unknown Data** (you'll see an example of how this can be done in the next section of this chapter). The data scientist then performs an analysis of the data and manually calculates results. Once the expected or correct results are established, they can be compared to the statistical model-produced results (using that separate unknown subset of data).

 The preceding is one round. Multiple rounds would be performed and the compared results would then be averaged and reviewed, eventually providing a fair estimate of a model's prediction performance.

Let's think of a real-world use case.

In `Chapter 6`, *Regularization for Database Improvement*, we again reviewed some sample data consisting of consulting project results. In that example, we explored the relationship between the total hours billed to the project, the total project management hours spent on the project, and the project's supposed profitability.

Looking back at that data to illustrate a point here, we can consider the various project characteristics (rather than variables):

- Was the project within the organization's core technology strength?
- Was there a full-time project manager assigned to the project?
- Was there a full-time client resource assigned to the project?
- Was the project work sub-contracted?
- Was the project a time and materials type of project?
- Was the project a not to exceed type of project?
- Was there a formal **quality assurance (QA)** part of the project?
- Was the work performed primarily on-site?
- Was the work performed primarily remote (from the customer site)?

Again, our predictive model wants to predict what characteristics a profitable consulting project had.

The following is a representation of the results of using a five-round cross-validation process to predict our model's expected accuracy:

Characteristic	Validation Percent	Round 1 Percent	Round 2 Percent	Round 3 Percent	Round 4 Percent	Round 5 Percent	Average
Core Technology	90%	90%	80%	89%	72%	90%	85%
FT Project Manage	37%	36%	37%	30%	35%	37%	35%
FT Client Resource	79%	78%	77%	79%	80%	78%	79%
Sub-Contracted	92%	9%	5%	15%	44%	79%	41%
Time & Materials	69%	99%	99%	89%	79%	99%	89%
Not to Exceed	90%	69%	69%	69%	59%	70%	71%
Formal QA	99%	89%	89%	91%	92%	99%	93%
On-site	75%	78%	79%	81%	84%	88%	81%
Remote	89%	99%	99%	89%	99%	19%	82%

Given the preceding figure, I'd say our predictive model is expected to be very accurate!

In summary, cross-validation combines (averages) measures of fit (prediction error) to derive a more accurate estimate of model prediction performance. This method is typically used in cases where there is not enough data available to test without losing significant modeling or testing quality.

Let's now move on to the final section of this chapter and look at some assessment examples using the R programming language.

R and statistical assessment

So, let's get started with some statistical assessment work!

As we discussed in the previous section, instead of using all the data (the entire population of observations) to train a statistical model (and then test using some of that data), cross-validation divides the data into training and testing datasets.

The first step that a data scientist needs to take when he or she is interested in using cross-validation to assess the performance of a statistical model is to organize (or split) the data into two separate subsets.

There are actually several approaches of cross-validation:

- **Leave-one-out cross-validation (LOOCV)**
- Holdout
- k-fold and repeated k-fold
- Re-substitution (most agree that this method is the simplest method)

This cross-validation approaches all focus on how to split the data for the training, testing, and validation. Each has its own merit (pros and cons).

There are (as always) many approaches to programming a problem. The following is one such simple method. This example randomly splits the total file using a 70 to 30 split:

```
# --- setting seed so we get same data split each time
# --- we'll use 100 for seed
set.seed(100)
# --- determine the total number of rows in the data
# --- using nrow function
nall = nrow(MyData)
# --- number of rows for train subset is 70%
# --- of the total rowsntrain = floor(0.7 * nall)
```

```
# --- number of rows for test subset is 30%
# --- of the total rows
ntest = floor(0.3* nall)
index = seq(1:nall)
# --- create the train data subsettrainIndex = sample(index, ntrain)
testIndex = index[-train]
train = mydata[trainIndex,]
test = mydata[test,]
```

Once we have created the files we want, we can proceed with training and validate our statistical model.

 As we have mentioned from time to time throughout this book, a proven practice is to save the preceding code so that it can be used again and again with new datasets.

Questions to ask

In the previous sections of this chapter, we discussed the various approaches or methods for cross-validation, the number of rounds of cross-validation (in fact, we showed the results of a five-round cross validation effort), as well as how to organize and split the data for the purpose of performing cross-validation on a statistical model.

Before proceeding with the cross-validation process, a number of points need to be considered. (A plan is created!) This brings up the following questions:

1. Which method or approach for cross-validation should I use? The answer is the method that is the best. Then again a new question arises—what does best mean? Each approach has its own strengths and weaknesses. The best cross-validation approach is one that best suits your data and objectives. More often than not, which approach you should use may not be revealed until other approaches are attempted.

2. What is the appropriate number of rounds or folds one should be performing? Usually, the more the better! However, this will be determined by factors such as which cross-validation approach you choose to use and the amount of available data and time.

3. What is the method to create each of the round's data? Again, this will be determined by factors such as the cross-validation approach you choose to use, the amount of available data and time, and the data scientist's abilities!

Learning curves

Another method of assessing a statistical model's performance is by evaluating the model's growth of learning or the model's ability to improve learning (obtain a better score) with additional experience (for example, more rounds of cross-validation).

The phrase, **with additional experience**, is vitally important in statistics as we not only look for a statistical model to perform well on a given population of data, but we hope that the model's performance will improve as it is trained and tested on more and more data.

The information indicating a model's performance, result, or score with a data file population is usually combined with other scores to show a line or curve—this is known as the statistical model's learning curve.

This means that the learning curve is a graphical representation of the growth of learning (the scores shown in a vertical axis) with practice (the individual data files or rounds shown in the horizontal axis).

This can also be conceptualized as follows:

- The same task repeated in a series
- A body of knowledge learned over time

Example of a learning curve

For illustration, suppose we wanted to visualize the rate of growth of learning of a statistical model over multiple rounds of performance results, comparing test versus training data for a selected characteristic.

This was shown in an earlier section of this chapter:

Characteristic	Validation Percent	Round 1 Percent	Round 2 Percent	Round 3 Percent	Round 4 Percent	Round 5 Percent	Average
Core Technology	90%	90%	80%	89%	72%	90%	85%
FT Project Manage	37%	36%	37%	30%	35%	37%	35%
FT Client Resource	79%	78%	77%	79%	80%	78%	79%
Sub-Contracted	92%	9%	5%	15%	44%	79%	41%
Time & Materials	69%	99%	99%	89%	79%	99%	89%
Not to Exceed	90%	69%	69%	69%	59%	70%	71%
Formal QA	99%	89%	89%	91%	92%	99%	93%
On-site	75%	78%	79%	81%	84%	88%	81%
Remote	89%	99%	99%	89%	99%	19%	82%

The following is a visualization showing the learning curve that indicates the rate of learning of a predictive model using the preceding resultant scores of cross-validation rounds for the selected characteristic:

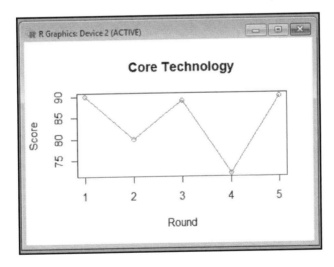

Core Technology

The following is the sample R code that generated the preceding visualization:

```
# --- load scores from 5 rounds of testing
v <-c(90,80, 89,72, 90)
# -- plot the model scores round by round
plot(v, type = "o", col = "red", xlab = "Round", ylab = "Score", main =
"Core Technology")
```

Again, learning curves relating a statistical model's performance to experience are commonly found to be used when performing model assessments, especially when performing many rounds of tests (or in an analysis effort to determine the correct cross-validation method to use on a statistical model).

To this point, simply performing the rounds of testing and then reviewing the results is not quite enough. A seasoned data scientist will make sure to properly document each iteration of the testing, along with its corresponding results and conclusions.

Looking again at the preceding example, we can add to use of the R function png, which can be used to automatically create and save an image file of any visualization you create during the assessment processing that you do. If you predefine a file structure to save your assessment results and this or a similar approach, it will save much time later.

 The R function png can easily be converted to many other bitmap formats, and both can be displayed in modern web browsers!

The following is our example R code statements that show the setup of the data, the creation of an image file, and the generation of the plot visualization:

```
# --- load scores from 5 rounds of testing
v <-c(90,80, 89,72, 90)
# -- create an image file for the visualization for later use
png(file = "c:/provenpratice/learning curve.png", type = c("windows",
"cairo", "cairo-png"))
# -- plot the model scores round by round
plot(v, type = "o", col = "red", xlab = "Round", ylab = "Score", main =
"Learning Curve")
# -- close output
dev.off()
```

You should note that, if you're expecting an interactive result, you won't receive it! The preceding code uses png and this simply writes the output (of the plot function) to that file.

Good practice advice: use the `dev.off()` to make sure that the file is closed.

This creates the following graphic as a file:

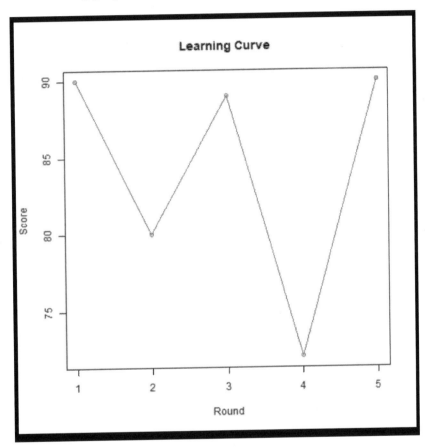

Summary

In this chapter, we defined assessment and then examined the similarities and differences between assessment and statistical assessment. Next, we covered development versus assessment and then explained how data assessment and data quality assurance have some overlap, and go hand in hand, but also have different objectives. Finally, we applied the idea of statistical assessment using the programming tool R.

In the next chapter, we will define the neural network model and draw from a developer's knowledge of data models to help understand the purpose and use of neural networks in data science.

9
Databases and Neural Networks

In this chapter, we will look at and define **Artificial Neural Network (ANN)** and draw data from a data developer's knowledge of data, databases, and data models to help him or she understand the purpose and use of neural networks, and why neural networks are so significant to data science and statistics.

We have organized the information in this chapter into the following key areas:

- Definition of a neural network
- Relating a neural network model to a database model
- Looking at R-based neural networks
- Use cases

Ask any data scientist

Today, if you ask any data scientist about the statistical methods, (or even a few) you will most likely discover that there are two most well-known statistical methods used within the practice of data science and the statistics industry today for predictive modeling. We introduced these two methods in Chapter 6, *Database Progression to Database Regression.*

These two methods are as follows:

- Linear regression
- Logistic regression

The **linear regression** method is probably considered to be the *classic* or most common starting point for problems, where the goal is to predict a numerical quantity. The **Linear Regression** (or **LR**) model is based on a linear combination of input features.

The **logistic regression** method uses a nonlinear transformation of this linear feature combination in order to restrict the range of the output in the interval [0, 1]. In doing so, it predicts the probability that the output belongs to one of two classes. Thus, it is a very well-known technique for classification.

Recall that classification is the process of recognizing to which set of categories (or sub-populations) a new or different observation belongs, on the basis of a training set of data.

Both of these methods have their individual strengths, but both also share the same disadvantage in that they are not very good at predicting if they have to deal with the situation of a high volume of input features.

In this chapter (as an alternative to linear and logistic regression), we want to introduce the concept of ANNs, which is technically a nonlinear approach to solving both regression and classification problems.

They (ANNs) are significantly more robust when dealing with a higher dimensional input feature space and, for classification, they possess a **natural** way to handle more than two output classes. We'll talk more about the advantages of ANNs later in this chapter.

Artificial neural networks are a **biologically inspired** statistical method or model (based on the structure and functions of biological neural networks), with their roots dating all the way back to the 1940s.

Another interesting viewpoint:

> *Neural Networks are a machine learning framework that attempts to mimic the learning pattern of natural biological neural networks.*
>
> *- Jose Portilla, Udemy Data Science Instructor.*

Interest in artificial neural networks has varied greatly since then--mostly because the first artificial neural network models were very rudimentary and therefore found to be limited in practice compared to the expectations at the time.

*Neural networks have not always been popular, partly because they were, and still are in some cases, computationally expensive and partly because they did not seem to yield better results when compared with simpler methods such as **support vector machines** (SVMs). Nevertheless, neural networks have, once again, raised attention and become popular.*
-Michy Alice, September 2015.

Furthermore, training a large artificial neural network does necessitate substantial computational resources. Recently, there has been a huge resurgence in the interest in artificial neural networks as distributed on-demand computing resources are now becoming widespread, and an important area of machine learning, known as **deep learning**, is already extremely popular and showing great promise.

The timing is right!

For this reason, it is a great time for a data developer to begin learning about ANNs models.

Deep learning (also known as **deep structured learning, hierarchical learning**, or **deep machine learning**) is a class of machine learning algorithms that use a cascade of many layers of nonlinear processing units for feature extraction and transformation (`en.wikipedia.org/wiki/Deep_learning`).

Let's get started!

Defining neural network

Our approach is to always start with a solid definition. So--what exactly is an artificial neural network? Perhaps:

A computer system modeled on the human brain and nervous system.

A popular understanding or, if we check online for a definition:

In machine learning and cognitive science, artificial neural networks (ANNs) are a family of models inspired by biological neural networks (the central nervous systems of animals, in particular, the brain) and are used to estimate or approximate functions that can depend on a large number of inputs and are generally unknown.

So there are many definitions, but in summarization, the common theme through all of the definitions you'll find for an ANNs is that it is defined as a computer data model based upon the concepts of how a human brain works.

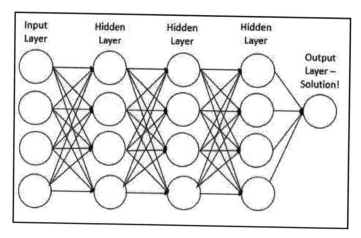

ANN model representation

As the preceding screenshot suggests, the construction of a typical artificial neural network is based on some number of the following:

- Nodes
- Layers
- Connections

Nodes

Each of the layers is made up of a number of interconnected nodes--each node containing what is referred to as an **activation function**.

There will be at least one node in the input layer for each predictor variable that exists within the data. The input nodes feed the input values (the **problem to be solved**) to each of the nodes in the (next) hidden layer.

The input(s) to each node are summed to give a single value, x. This is then inputted to the node's activation function, and the output of the node is the output of its activation function, $f(x)$.

There are a number of functions that can be used in artificial neural network nodes, including the radial basis function or a simple linear function, but the most common is the sigmoid or logistic function.

A sigmoid function is typically the most common and perhaps easiest to understand. The sigmoid function is a mathematical function having a characteristic S-shaped curve or sigmoid curve. Sigmoid functions have a domain of all real numbers, with the return value monotonically increasing most often from 0 to 1 or alternatively from –1 to 1, depending on convention. (`https://en.wikipedia.org/wiki/Sigmoid_function`)

The nodes within an artificial neural network will always produce or calculate a value between 0 and 1, so the output of a node can only ever be in the collection 0 to 1.

Layers

The **layer** is a universal term used to define a collection of **nodes** operating together at a specific depth within an artificial neural network.

Hidden layers will have a variable number of nodes (determined by the training algorithm used). Each of those nodes will contain numerous functions with logic to process the inputs and calculate a result. The resulting value is then passed to the next layer.

The layer summary is as follows:

- **Input layer**: This contains your data, with one node per variable
- **Hidden layer(s)**: Each layer attempts to learn a different aspect about your data by minimizing an error/cost function
- **Output layer**: This is the simplest layer, usually consisting of a single output for classification problems

Training

Recalling from the previous section describing artificial neural network nodes, if all the nodes work the same way or, at least produce the same result (0 or 1), how does the network differentiate between classes?

It uses assigned weights to each node's inputs. This is a feature (or variable in the data) that can have a large or small weighting, which then results in varying the contribution that the variable or feature makes to the *sum* in any node.

In practice, a variable can be assigned a large weight feeding into one node and an almost zero weight feeding into another node, which would mean that the variable would have a strong influence on the first and practically none on the second.

The sigmoid function (which we also mentioned in the previous section) indicates that the node's output switches from a zero to a one when its x value crosses a threshold. This can transpire in numerous ways, such as if one highly weighted input has a high value or if a collection of medium-weighted inputs have high values.

Training the artificial neural network is the process of systematically discovering the best values of weights to maximize the accurateness of classification.

Solution

The value coming out of a node in the hidden layer is multiplied by a weight associated with the node that did the calculation and adds to the weighted values of other nodes. This summation becomes the artificial neural network model's output or solution. (Observe that the term used for this varies between data scientists, some say output, others solution, result, or even outcome).

Again, the problems are presented to the artificial neural network (through the model's input layer), which will communicate to one or (most likely) more hidden layers where the actual processing is done via a system of weighted connections. The hidden layers then link to an output layer where the solution is given.

Most artificial neural network models contain some form of an algorithm that governs how the model **learns**. This is the algorithm that we discussed earlier as the process that **adjusts the weights** of the node connections according to the (input) problems that have been submitted to it.

This **adjusting of the node's weights** (some call **right-regulating**) is similar to the idea of learning to recognize an image (or **determining a solution**) based on experience (in this case, the experience might be reviewing example after example).

Understanding the concepts

To gain an understanding of a new concept, it always helps to draw similarities between the familiar and the new.

To that point, to better comprehend the notion of artificial neural networks, it would be helpful for us to compare the concepts of ANNs to how a conventional database algorithm processes data and information (or how it works).

In the next section, we will compare concepts concerning artificial neural network models to those of common data or database models.

Neural network models and database models

As we noted in the previous section of this chapter, neural network models are a **system of processing nodes**, interconnected across layers that do not process data in a sequential manner. How does this scheme compare to a conventional database model or program?

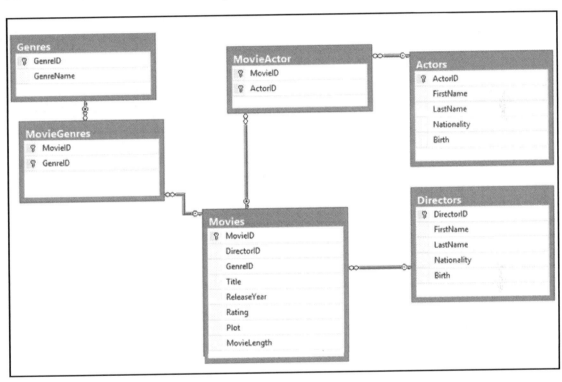

A conventional database model representation

As we noted in the previous section of this chapter, neural network models are a **system of processing nodes**, interconnected across layers that do not process data in a sequential manner. How does this scheme compare to a conventional database model or program?

In the technology industry, a conventional (database) model is sometimes called a **serial processing component**, which means that this type of model has a central processing unit or CPU (perhaps you can think of this as a large, central *processing node*) that accesses raw data and instructions (already stored in memory).

In a conventional database model, the central processor carries out calculations or logic (an algorithm) on input or selected data, stores the calculated results (in a specified memory location), then goes on to the next instruction (and data), and so on—until a solution or result is reached.

This idea is somewhat analogous to the concept of a solitary processing *stream* within a neural network:

- A node accepts or consumes data
- A node applies logic
- A node outputs its results

Similar, but keep in mind that conventional database models are serial in that they perform each task (or instruction) in a linear, or one after the other, fashion, while multiple node streams within an artificial neural network model perform tasks in parallel.

So, in a serial system, the computational steps are deterministic, sequential, and logical, and the state of a given variable can be tracked from one operation to another. In comparison, ANNs are not sequential or necessarily deterministic.

There are other key differences, which include the following notions which are explained in the following sub-sections.

No single or main node

Rather than a single, complex central processor (or node), there are many simple nodes-- which generally do nothing more than taking the weighted sum of their inputs from other nodes.

Not serial

ANNs do not execute programmed instructions linearly or serially; they respond in parallel (either simulated or actual) to the inputs presented to them.

No memory address to store results

There are also no separate memory addresses to store data within an artificial neural network model.

Instead, information is contained in the overall activation *state* of the model. **Knowledge** is therefore represented by the artificial neural network model itself, which is quite literally more than the sum of its individual components.

As a final point, for the data developer, the notion of an artificial neural network might be imagined as **kicking-off** and running multiple SQL queries asynchronously. Imagine creating a SQL **DTS (Data Transformation Services)** or **SQL Server Integration Services (SSIS)** package with a simple branching task flow so that DTS will launch tasks in individual **spids (Server Process ID)**. Each of the spids then would align to the idea of a neural network node stream, all working in parallel to create a result or solution.

A very good explanation of how a neural network works--using a data developer-type practical example—can be found online authored by Sunil Ray.

 Understanding and coding Neural Networks from Scratch in Python and R, which, as of writing this, can be found at `www.analyticsvidhya.com` under: `/blog/2017/05/neural-network-from-scratch-in-python-and-r`.

He terms the following quote:

"If you have been a developer or seen one work you know how it is to search for bugs in a code. You would fire various test cases by varying the inputs or circumstances and look for the output. The change in output provides you a hint on where to look for the bug--which module to check, which lines to read. Once you find it, you make the changes and the exercise continues until you have the right code/application.

Neural networks work in very similar manner. It takes several input, processes it through multiple neurons from multiple hidden layers and returns the result using an output layer. This result estimation process is technically known as Forward Propagation.

Next, we compare the result with actual output. The task is to make the output to neural network as close to actual (desired) output. Each of these neurons are contributing some error to final output. How do you reduce the error?

We try to minimize the value/ weight of neurons those are contributing more to the error and this happens while traveling back to the neurons of the neural network and finding where the error lies. This process is known as Backward Propagation."

Okay, that was a lot to take in--but now that we, with any luck, have a respectable understanding of what an artificial neural network is and how it works, let's look at ANNs and the R programming language.

R-based neural networks

Now that we know a bit about how artificial neural networks work, let's review some fundamental information on how to implement one with the R programming language.

R-based ANN packages

The idea here is not to give a detailed step-by-step instruction manual on how to create an intricate and powerful ANN, but more to show how one can easily create an ANN model using R—with literally only basic R skills or experience.

References

Yes, you will find that there is plenty of respectable, easy-to-understand, and valuable information and examples on artificial neural networks generously obtainable on the internet.

One such resource is offered by Gekko Quant (`http://gekkoquant.com/author/gekkoquant/`) and is worth taking some time to locate and read.

This information offers a very nice tutorial that produces an artificial neural network that takes a single input (a number that you want to calculate a square root for) and produces a single output (the square root of the number input).

The output of this artificial neural network example model is nicely displayed in an easy-to-understand format and I'll show it here as a great example of how the results of an ANN model should look:

Input	Expected Output	Neural Net Output
1	1	0.9623402772
4	2	2.0083461217
9	3	2.9958221776
16	4	4.0009548085
25	5	5.0028838579
36	6	5.9975810435
49	7	6.9968278722
64	8	8.0070028670
81	9	9.0019220736
100	10	9.9222007864

Results of an ANN

From the output information shown here, you can see (as the author declares) that the neural network does a reasonable job at finding the square root (of each input number).

Before a data scientist can begin the process of fitting an artificial neural network, some important time-saving groundwork needs to be accomplished, which we'll discuss in the next few sections.

To be sure, artificial neural networks are not easy to understand, train, and tune; some preparatory or preprocessing first is strongly recommended.

Data prep and preprocessing

Let's start with the obvious—our data!

The more experience a data scientist gains with working with ANN models, the more he or she will come to understand the importance of formally reviewing and preparing the data ahead of he or she can begin attempting to train or fit the model.

We discussed data cleaning in Chapter 3, *A Developer Approach to Data Cleaning*, so you should have a good understanding of the importance of and the process of data cleaning and cleansing at this point, so we'll focus here on some data preparation efforts more specific to our topic of artificial neural network models.

It is a popular opinion among data scientists that it may be good practice to normalize your data before training an artificial neural network on it. Depending on your data, not performing any data normalization may lead to unusable results or at least to a very difficult training process; most of the time, the algorithm will not converge before the number of maximum iterations allowed--in other words, it runs out of attempts!

Based on industry experience, the artificial neural network may have difficulty converging before the maximum number of iterations allowed if the data is not normalized.

Although there are numerous and diverse methods to accomplish normalization or normalizing of your data, one of the most universally used is the R built-in `scale()` function, which can easily accomplish this task.

The scale function is a generic R function whose default method centers and/or scales (normalized) the columns of a numeric matrix for you.

I like the following scale example using simple R code statements because it makes it obvious that the scale function works correctly (as expected?) and is a lot more effective than attempting to perform *manual* scaling, that is, writing the R code statements to scale the values.

Take a quick look:

```
Setting up the sample data, in the object named "x":
# --- set up the data
Set.seed(1)
X <- runif(7)
Next, here is the manual scaling approach, using mean and sd:
#---manual scale method
(x - mean(x)) /sd(x)
And then the use of the R scale function:
# --- scale using the function
Scale(x)
```

Finally, here is the output, showing the same results produced out of both the manual scale approach as well as out of the scale function:

```
R Console                                            [-] [□] [✕]

>      set.seed(1)
>      x <- runif(7)
>
>      # Manually scaling
>      (x - mean(x)) / sd(x)
[1] -1.01951259013 -0.68940037389 -0.06788275305  0.97047345797 -1.21713897716
[6]  0.94007370915  1.08338752711
>
>      scale(x)
                 [,1]
[1,] -1.01951259013
[2,] -0.68940037389
[3,] -0.06788275305
[4,]  0.97047345797
[5,] -1.21713897716
[6,]  0.94007370915
[7,]  1.08338752711
attr(,"scaled:center")
[1] 0.5947772287
attr(,"scaled:scale")
[1] 0.3229666497
>
```

Awesome!

Data splitting

The next step in our preprocessing is *splitting the data*. We covered data *splitting* in detail in Chapter 8, *Database Development and Assessment*, so we won't revisit the topic here.

However, recall that the process of data splitting will have the objective of creating both a training subset of data as well as a testing subset of data, from the original dataset or source (based on appropriate logic).

For example, we could accomplish our data split by *randomly* splitting the data into a train and a test set, then fit a linear regression model and test it on the test dataset (or use the split method we used in the last chapter, to create a 70/30 split of our data).

Model parameters

There is no best practice or recommended rule or policy that will tell the data scientist how many layers and/or nodes to use (although there are several more or less industry--accepted rules) in an artificial neural network model.

Customarily, if at all necessary, one hidden layer is enough for most or, a vast number of, artificial neural network statistical applications (although you may have observed that we showed three hidden layers in our graphical image at the beginning of this chapter).

As far as the number of nodes, the number should frequently be between the input layer size and the output layer size, usually 2/3 of the input size.

Bottom line—when the data scientist is determining the number of layers and nodes to have in his or her artificial neural network model, they will test, test, and test again (and again and again) to find the best or most optimal solution to meet the current requirements, as there is no guarantee that any past experience or *rules* will fit your statistical model best.

Cross-validation

Cross-validation is an important topic that we introduced in Chapter 2, *Declaring the Objectives*, and again we recall that it IS a very important step in building any predictive model.

While there are many different kinds of cross-validation methods, the basic idea is a data scientist repeating the following process a number of times:

Train me, test me, split me:

1. Do the train-test split.
2. Fit the model to the train set.
3. Test the model on the test set.
4. Calculate and review the prediction error.
5. Repeat (*n* number of times).

By conducting the preceding process a number of times, the data scientist will then be able to calculate the average error that is then used to assess how the statistical model is performing (performance is another important topic, one which we discussed in Chapter 8, *Database Development and Assessment*).

R packages for ANN development

So, how can a data scientist create his or her own **artificial neural network (ANN)**?

The R programming language provides (as of writing this) a nice variety of packages to create various types of artificial neural networks. These packages currently include the following.

ANN

This package provides a feed-forward artificial neural network optimized by **genetic algorithm (GA)**.

ANN2

This provides the training of general classification and regression neural networks using gradient descent.

NNET

The package NNET created by Ripley provides methods to use feedforward neural networks with a single hidden layer and for multinomial log-linear models. Specifically, this chapter of the book will portray the NNET method. Here, we have briefly described the method and parameters used.

Note that I am splitting the data in this way: 90% train set and 10% test set in a random way for 10 times.

I am also initializing a progress bar using the `plyr` library because I want to keep an eye on the status of the process as the fitting of the neural network may take a while.

Black boxes

ANNs can be very challenging to comprehend (even for the most advanced or seasoned data scientist). Explaining their outcome (or results) is much more demanding than explaining the outcome of a simpler model such as a linear model.

Sometimes, data scientists will understand an artificial neural network model at only a very high level. Although one can have only this level of understanding and still be able to be productive, not fully understanding the interworkings of artificial neural network models can result in a situation referred to as a **BBU** model or **black box understood model** or method.

 A black box model, method, or system is one that can be viewed in terms of its inputs and outputs, without any knowledge of its internal workings.

Consequently, depending on the kind of application you need, you might want to keep in mind that you will have to properly explain the results of the model (not just run the model and producing a result) before the results can be useful, and therefore invest the time in gaining a proper, detailed understanding of the model and methods being used.

A use case

It has been said (most likely not by a data scientist!) that:

A neural network model cannot learn anything that a reasonably intelligent human could not learn given enough time from the same data.

The key term in this statement is enough time. Data scientists (and human beings in general) almost never, ever have the luxury of enough time--and time may be the difference between your organization's success and the competition.

In defense of using artificial neural networks (rather than a *reasonably intelligent* human) are some of the following additional advantages of artificial neural network models:

- Make discoveries no one has even imagined yet
- Find solutions in much less time than even a team of people
- Produce results at a much lower cost
- Produce consistent results with the inputs they've been trained on and should generalize well if tweaked properly
- NNs never get bored or distracted

With all of these advantages, let's consider some practical use case scenarios for artificial neural network models.

Popular use cases

There are many uses for artificial neural networks. Surveying the industry, the most established artificial neural network use cases are the following applications.

Character recognition

Neural networks can be used to recognize handwritten characters, converting handwriting in real time to control a computer or for **automatic number-plate recognition (ANPR)** to automatically read vehicle registration plates.

Image compression

Neural networks can receive and process enormous amounts of information at once, making them useful in image compression. With the explosion of big data, applying ANN to digital images in order to reduce their cost for storage or transmission is a growing opportunity.

Stock market prediction

The real-time movements of the stock market are extremely complicated due to the influence of a large number of factors. Many factors weigh in like high, low, open and close price, volume, the price of other securities as well as economic indicators. As neural networks can scrutinize large amounts of information rapidly, they can be used to predict stock prices.

Fraud detection

In recent years, the development of new technologies has also provided further ways in which criminals may commit fraud. Neural networks can learn suspicious patterns from samples to detect approximate classes, clusters, or patterns of suspicious behaviour and use them later to detect frauds.

Neuroscience

Theoretical and computational neuroscience is the study of theoretical analysis and the computational modeling of biological neural systems. As neural systems attempt to replicate cognitive processes and behaviour, the field is closely related to cognitive and behavioural modeling.

Summary

In this chapter, we defined neural networks and, from a data developer's knowledge of databases and data models, grew to understand the purpose and use of neural networks and why neural networks are so important to data science. We also looked at an R-based ANN and listed some popular use case examples.

In the next chapter, we will introduce the idea of using statistical boosting to better understand data in a database.

10
Boosting your Database

In this chapter, we will explain what statistical boosting is, how it works, and introduce the notion of using statistical boosting to better understand data in a database.

We have again broken the subjects in this chapter down into the following important areas for clarity:

- Definition and purpose of statistical boosting
- What you can learn from boosting (to help) your database
- Using R to illustrate boosting methods

Definition and purpose

First, we can consider a common definition you may find online:

> *Boosting is a machine learning ensemble meta-algorithm for primarily reducing bias, and also variance in supervised learning, and a family of machine learning algorithms which convert weak learners to strong ones.*
>
> *-Wikipedia*
>
> https://en.wikipedia.org/wiki/Boosting_(machine_learning)

 Reminder: In statistics, ensemble methods use multiple learning algorithms to obtain better predictive performance than could be obtained from any of the fundamental or basic learning algorithms (although results vary by data and data model).

Before we head into the details behind statistical boosting, it is imperative that we take some time here to first understand bias, variance, noise, and what is meant by a weak learner, and a strong learner.

The following sections will cover these terms and related concepts.

Bias

Let's start out with a discussion on the statistical bias.

A statistic is biased if it is calculated in such a way that it is analytically dissimilar to the population parameter being estimated.

One of the best explanations for bias that I've come across is the concept of a scale that is off zero by a small amount. In this scenario, the scale will give slightly over-estimated results. In other words, when someone steps on the scale, the total weight may be over or understated (which might make that person conclude that the diet they are on is working better than it really is).

In statistics, data scientists need to recognize that there are actually several categories that are routinely used to define statistical bias. The next section lists these categories of bias along with examples.

 Categorizing bias is somewhat subjective since some of the categories will seem to overlap.

Categorizing bias

There are many categories of bias, including the following specific examples:

- **Selection bias**: This is when individual observations are more likely to be selected for study than others.
- **Spectrum bias**: This occurs when data scientists evaluate results on biased samples, leading to an overestimate of the sensitivity and specificity of the test(s).
- **Estimator bias**: This is the difference between an estimator's expected value and the true value of the parameter being estimated.
- **Omitted-variable bias**: This bias will occur in estimating the parameters in a regression analysis when the assumed specification neglects an independent variable.
- **Detection bias**: This occurs when a character or event is more likely to be observed for a particular set of study subjects.
- **Sampling bias**: This bias occurs when a statistical error is imposed due to an error in the sampling data.
- **Measurement bias**: This occurs then there is a systematic problem with test content, testing administration, and/or scoring procedures.
- **Funding bias**: This type of bias can lead to a selection of specific outcomes, observations, test samples, or test procedures that favor a study's financial sponsor.
- **Reporting bias**: Bias of this type involves askew in the availability of data, which causes observations of a certain type or collection to be more likely to be reported as a result or to affect performance.
- **Analytical bias**: This occurs based on the method or process used to evaluate the results of certain observations or the performance of a statistical model as a whole.
- **Exclusion bias**: This category of bias may arise based upon a process or procedure that has the potential to systematically exclude certain samples or observations from a statistical study.
- **Attrition bias**: When participants in a study or statistical project leave the program or process. In other words, a group or category of a project may leave or be removed and will no longer be considered by data scientists.
- **Recall bias**: When the accuracy or completeness of a study's participants does not align due to misrecollections of past events or characteristics of what is being studied. This results in an over-estimation or under-estimation of the results.

- **Observer bias**: This type of bias occurs when the researcher subconsciously influences the data due to cognitive bias, where judgment may alter how an observation or study is carried out/how results are recorded.
- **Confounding bias**: This type of bias occurs when factors affecting the same information in a study are misleading or otherwise confusing to the researcher or data scientist.
- **Negativity bias**: This occurs when a data scientist is inclined to give more weight or value to negative characteristics, events, or outcomes, just because they are negative.
- **Representative bias**: This occurs when data scientists take something for granted based upon certain observed characteristics identified within a group or certain observations.
- **Recency bias**: This category of bias occurs when the recent experiences and observations of a data scientist are used (or are given more value) to predict future outcomes.

And one of my favorite types:

- **Data-snooping bias**: This happens when the data scientist forms an incorrect opinion or makes a hypothesis, then proceeds to mine data that is especially in defense of that notion.

Causes of bias

Bias is a term that you will find is commonly thrown around in the field of statistics and, almost always, bias is equivalent to (or with) a negative or bad incident. In fact, even beyond the realm of statistics, bias almost always results in trouble or some form of distress.

Consider bias as favoritism. Favoritism that is present in the data collection process, for example, will typically result in misleading results or incorrect assumptions.

Bias can arise in various ways and, as a data scientist, one must be familiar with these occasions. Actually, bias can be introduced to a statistical project at any time or phase.

One of the most common times that bias is introduced is at the very start or beginning of a project when data is collected or selected. This is the worst, as almost every effort and all work completed afterwards will be suspect or, most likely, incorrect.

Bias data collection

A major source of bias is the way data is collected. Frankly, researchers who are inexperienced, or hoping for a certain result, may use inferior data collection methods or practices or actually collect data in ways that expose a particular emphasis or lead to an anticipated or expected result.

Some things to look for in data collection methods:

- Surveys that are constructed with a particular slant or emphasis
- Choosing a known group with a particular background to respond to a survey
- The reporting of data in misleading categorical groupings
- A non-randomness sample selection
- Systematic measurement errors

Bias sample selection

The process of sample selection or sampling is also subject to the introduction of bias. Sample bias occurs when the sample does not accurately represent a population. The bias that results from an unrepresentative sample is called **selection bias**.

Issues that can result in introducing bias to a statistical sample include:

- The timing of taking the sample
- The length or size of the sample
- The level of difficulty of the question
- Undercoverage (of the population)
- Nonresponses incorrectly used in a sample
- Voluntary responses incorrectly used within a sample
- The manner (in which the subjects in the sample were contacted (phone, mail, door-to-door, and so on), or how the observation data was split)

Enough about bias. Let's move on to the next section, where we will cover statistical variance.

Variance

In statistical theory (https://en.wikipedia.org/wiki/Statistics), the concept of variance is defined as follows:

The expectation (https://en.wikipedia.org/wiki/Expected_value) of the squared deviation of a random variable from its mean or, in other words, it is a measurement of just how far a set of random numbers are spread out from their average value.

The practice of the analysis of variance (or simply variance analysis) involves a data scientist evaluating the difference between two figures. Typically, this process applies financial or operational data in an attempt to identify and determine the cause of the variance. In applied statistics, there are different forms of variance analysis.

Variance and the analysis of variance is a big topic within the field and study of statistics, where it plays a key role in the following statistical practices:

- Descriptive statistics (https://en.wikipedia.org/wiki/Descriptive_statistics)
- Goodness of fit (https://en.wikipedia.org/wiki/Goodness_of_fit)
- Hypothesis testing (https://en.wikipedia.org/wiki/Statistical_hypothesis_testing)
- Monte Carlo sampling (https://en.wikipedia.org/wiki/Monte_Carlo_method)
- Statistical inference (https://en.wikipedia.org/wiki/Statistical_inference)

You'll find the following to be true with variance:

- Whenever there is a need for the statistical analysis of data, a data scientist will more than likely start with the process of variance analysis
- Statistical variance provides data scientists with a measuring stick to gauge how the data distributes itself (about the mean or an expected value)
- Unlike range (which only looks at extreme values), variance looks at all the data points and concludes their distribution

ANOVA

As a data scientist, when you are speaking about the process or practice of **analysis of variance**, you are speaking of **ANOVA**. ANOVA can be understood as an assortment of methods that are used in the investigation of found or potential differences (variances) amongst group means and their accompanying procedures.

ANOVA is studied and used in the field of statistics in three distinct styles. These styles are determined and defined by the number of independent variables a data scientist is working with or interested in:

- One-way ANOVA (deals with just one independent variable)
- Two-way ANOVA (uses or focuses on two independent variables)
- N-way ANOVA (when the data scientist is interested in more than two independent variables)

When a data scientist or researcher conducts an ANOVA, they are endeavoring to conclude whether there is a statistically significant difference between groups within their population. If they find that there is a difference, they will then go on to determine where the group differences are.

Noise

Noise or, to the data scientist, statistical noise, is the popular expression for acknowledged amounts of unexplained variation or variability in a sample, population, or data source.

The actual use of the term *noise* can be traced to early signal processing, where it was coined as a way of referring to undesirable (electromagnetic) energy that was found to be degrading the quality of signals and data.

To the data or database developer, consider the example of running a simple database query to determine the performance of a particular sales region of an organization. If your SQL query returns sales for every sales region, one might consider the additional sales regions—in the context of this exercise—noise that perhaps renders the sales information useless (again, in the context of trying to focus on a particular sales region). To resolve this condition, of course, one could restructure the query so that it filters out unwanted regions or manipulate the results of the query to remove the noise of unwanted regions. Keep in mind, in statistics, it may be unrealistic to recreate the data source.

Noisy data

Outside of statistics, people often use the term statistical noise to dismiss any data that they aren't interested in. An example of this is a professional football team's stadium, where fans cheering interferes with the ability of the visiting team to communicate. The noise is an inconvenience.

Within statistics though, when a data scientist acknowledges the presence of noise within a sample, it means that any results from statistical sampling might not be duplicated if the process were repeated. In this case, the sample may become noisy data and rendered meaningless because of the existence of too much variation.

The effort of unraveling the noise from the true signal has pretty much always been a major emphasis in statistics (so that the meaningful data could be used by researchers), however, the percentage of noisy data that is meaningful is often too insignificant to be of much use.

Over time, the term *noisy data* has grown to also refer to *any data that is not machine-readable*, such as unstructured text and even any data altered in some way that is no longer compatible with the program used to create it. Happily, advances in analytical tools are steadily overcoming these types of statistical obstacles (think IBM Watson analytics, but there are many others).

Some of the most commonly accepted examples of statistical noise include Gaussian noise, shot noise, and white noise. Enough of this noise about (statistical) noise!

Let's move on to learners.

Weak and strong learners

A nice segue (back) into the topic of boosting is a statistical algorithm or model's ability to improve its ability to predict overtime, that is, its performance.

If you are reading this book and have reached this section of this chapter, the assumption is that you understand the concept of machine learning, as it is related to statistical prediction-making. Learning is a computer or model's ability to learn (how to make predictions based upon data) without being explicitly programmed.

We use the term *explicitly* to mean *hardcoded* selections based upon data values.

If you build upon this concept, you can come to understand that a computer or model whose intention or objective is to make good predictions (to guess an outcome correctly) based upon data will perform or produce results that are somewhere between incorrect (bad) and correct (or good).

One can also then say that the computer or model could perhaps improve its performance with more experience (more data) and could improve learning at some rate.

Thus, a data scientist will label a computer or model (the learner) as a weak or strong learner, based on its performance (or its ability to predict or guess outcomes).

In the field of statistics and data science, one can also refer to a *learner* as a classifier or predictor.

So, what qualifies a learner as weak or strong?

A weak learner is one that, no matter what the data looks like (meaning the distribution of values within the data the model is being trained on), will always perform better than chance when it tries to label the data.

We qualify doing better than chance as always having an error rate which is less than half.

Weak to strong

Better than random guessing is fundamentally the one and only prerequisite for a weak learner. So, as long as an algorithm or model can consistently beat random guessing, applying a boosting algorithm will be able to increase the accuracy of the model's predictions (its performance) and consequently convert the model from being a weak learner to a strong learner.

Take note, data scientists agree that increasing a model's predictive ability or performance even to ever so slightly better than random guessing results means success.

When a data scientist considers the options for improving the performance of a model (or converting a weak learner to a strong learner), numerous factors need to be considered.

These factors include model bias, processing time, and complexity. Let's explain each a little.

Model bias

We talked about *statistical bias* in an earlier section of this chapter. The level of bias identified within a statistical model needs to be considered. Typically, the lower the amount of bias, the better, since some methods for improving on a weak learner—such as boosting—can overfit, resulting in misleading results.

Training and prediction time

Whether or not, the approach for improving a weak learner's performance adds significantly to the amount of time a model takes to learn, train, or predict on a data subset. Usually, the more you train a model, the better the results, so if you are anticipating requiring hundreds of training iterations, you need to consider how much longer that effort or process will take if your improvements increase the training iteration by 100%.

Complexity

Often, there is an assumption that a weak learner is computationally simple in design (it's a weak learner, right?), but that is not always the case. Understanding the level of complexity of an algorithm or model before choosing an approach for improving performance is critical in the decision-making process.

Which way?

Which way (which approach) a data scientist will go or take to improve a model's performance and convert it from a weak learner into a strong learner will ultimately depend on many factors, but in the end, the approach taken depends on the individual problem.

AdaBoost (also known as **Adaptive Boosting**) is an iterative algorithm using a designated number of iterations or rounds to improve on a weak learner. This algorithm starts by training/testing a weak learner on data, weighting each example equally. The examples which are misclassified get their weights increased for the next round(s), while those that are correctly classified get their weights decreased.

We will know about AdaBoost later in this chapter.

Back to boosting

At this point, we have covered all of the topics most pertinent to boosting, so let's now get back to the main event, statistical boosting.

We have already offered a description of what statistical boosting is and what it is used for (a learning algorithm intended to reduce bias and variance and convert weak learners into strong ones).

Key to this concept is the idea of how learners inherently behave, with a weak learner defined as one which is only slightly correlated with the true classification (it can label examples better than random guessing). In contrast, a strong learner is one that is well-correlated with the true classification.

How it started

Boosting an algorithm in an attempt to improve performance is, in reality, hypothetical. That is, it is a question every data scientist should ask for their statistical algorithm or model.

This is known in statistics as the hypothesis-boosting question and is all about the data scientist finding a way to even slightly improve a learning process (turning a weak learner into a strong(er) learner).

The idea of a strong learner only implies a slightly improved learner-- actually, only slightly better than random guessing.

In the data science or statistics world, the hypothesis-boosting question also implies the actual existence of an efficient algorithm that outputs a hypothesis of arbitrary accuracy for the problem being solved. These algorithms (that improve learners) have quickly become known simply as **boosting**.

As usual, data scientists interchangeably use terms to identify the same thing, and boosting is no different, as some data scientists will refer to boosting as *resampling* or *combining*.

AdaBoost

Back to our previous mention of a package named **AdaBoost**, which is short for **adaptive boosting**. AdaBoost is a boosting approach referred to as an *ensemble learning algorithm*. Ensemble learning is when multiple learners are used in conjunction with each other to build a stronger learning algorithm.

AdaBoost works by selecting a base algorithm and then iteratively improving it by accounting for the incorrectly classified examples in the training dataset.

 A wonderful explanation of boosting and AdaBoost can be found online: *Better living through AdaBoost* http://bbacon.org/Better-Living-Through-AdaBoost.

The aforementioned article describes how AdaBoost works:

- AdaBoost trains a model on a data subset
- Weak learners (based upon performance) are weighted
- The process is repeated

In narrative form, the AdaBoost boosting logic can be explained in the following way:

- The process works by building a model on training data and then measuring the results' accuracy on that training data, then:
    - The individual results that were erroneous in the model are assigned a larger weight (or weighted more) than those that were correct, and then the model is *retrained* again using these new weights. This logic is then repeated multiple times, adjusting the weights of individual observations each time based on whether they were correctly classified or not in the last iteration!

 The AdaBoost algorithm was originally offered by *Freund* and *Schapire* in the Journal of *Computer and System Sciences* in a 1997 paper titled *A Decision-Theoretic Generalization of On-Line Learning and an Application to Boosting*.

What you can learn from boosting (to help) your database

Thinking from the perspective or point of view of a database developer, you may be trying to conceptualize the process of boosting. As we've done throughout this book, here, we'll try to use a database-oriented example to help our understanding of boosting:

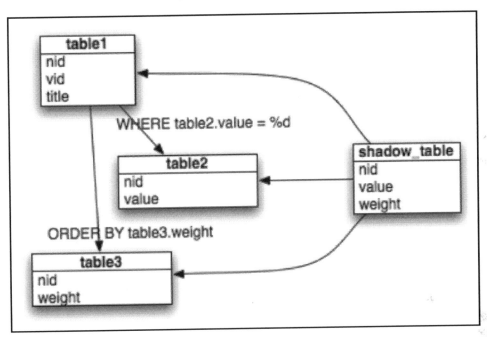

Our example starts with a relational database. There, effective indexes are one of the best ways to improve the performance of a database application. Without an effective (strong?) index, the database engine is like a reader trying to find a phrase within a reference book by having to take the time to examine each and every page. But if the reader uses the reference book's index, the reader can then complete the task in a much shorter time (better performance = better results).

In database terms, a table scan occurs when there is no available index identified to boost the performance of a database query. In a table scan, the database engine examines each and every row in the table to satisfy the query results.

One of the most important jobs for a database developer is finding the best index to use when generating an execution plan (for a query). Most major databases offer tools to show you execution plans for a query and help in optimizing and tuning query indexes.

The preceding situation might be compared to repetitively testing queries in a database, scoring individual performances (in returning the query results) until an efficient (or strong) index is determined.

This then has the effect of improving the performance of the database query so that it becomes a strong responder (or, if you will, a strong learner).

Using R to illustrate boosting methods

In order to further illustrate the use of boosting, we should have an example.

In this section, we'll take a high-level look at a thought-provoking prediction problem drawn from *Mastering Predictive Analytics with R, Second Edition*, James D. Miller and Rui Miguel Forte, August 2017 (`https://www.packtpub.com/big-data-and-business-intelligence/mastering-predictive-analytics-r-second-edition`).

In this original example, patterns made by radiation on a telescope camera are analyzed in an attempt to predict whether a certain pattern came from gamma rays leaking into the atmosphere or from regular background radiation.

Gamma rays leave distinctive elliptical patterns and so we can create a set of features to describe these. The dataset used is the *MAGIC Gamma Telescope Data Set*, hosted by the *UCI Machine Learning Repository* at `http://archive.ics.uci.edu/ml/datasets/MAGIC+Gamma+Telescope`.

This data consists of 19,020 observations, holding the following list of attributes:

Column name	Type	Definition
FLENGTH	Numerical	The major axis of the ellipse (mm)
FWIDTH	Numerical	The minor axis of the ellipse (mm)
FSIZE	Numerical	Logarithm to the base ten of the sum of the content of all pixels in the camera photo
FCONC	Numerical	Ratio of the sum of the two highest pixels over FSIZE
FCONC1	Numerical	Ratio of the highest pixel over FSIZE

FASYM	Numerical	Distance from the highest pixel to the centre, projected onto the major axis (mm)
FM3LONG	Numerical	Third root of the third moment along the major axis (mm)
FM3TRANS	Numerical	Third root of the third moment along the minor axis (mm)
FALPHA	Numerical	Angle of the major axis with the vector to the origin (degrees)
FDIST	Numerical	Distance from the origin to the centre of the ellipse (mm)
CLASS	Binary	Gamma rays (g) or Background Hadron Radiation (b)

Prepping the data

First, various steps need to be performed on our example data.

The data is first loaded into an R data frame object named `magic`, recoding the CLASS output variable to use classes 1 and −1 for gamma rays and background radiation respectively:

```
> magic <- read.csv("magic04.data", header = FALSE)
> names(magic) <- c("FLENGTH", "FWIDTH", "FSIZE", "FCONC", "FCONC1",
    "FASYM", "FM3LONG", "FM3TRANS", "FALPHA", "FDIST", "CLASS")
> magic$CLASS <- as.factor(ifelse(magic$CLASS =='g', 1, -1))
```

Next, the data is split into two files: a training data and a test data frame using an 80-20 split:

```
> library(caret)
> set.seed(33711209)
> magic_sampling_vector <- createDataPartition(magic$CLASS,
                         p = 0.80, list = FALSE)
> magic_train <- magic[magic_sampling_vector, 1:10]
> magic_train_output <- magic[magic_sampling_vector, 11]
> magic_test <- magic[-magic_sampling_vector, 1:10]
> magic_test_output <- magic[-magic_sampling_vector, 11]
```

The model used for boosting is a simple multilayer perceptron with a single hidden layer leveraging R's `nnet` package.

Neural networks, (covered in `Chapter 9`, *Databases and Neural Networks*) often produce higher accuracy when inputs are normalized, so, in this example, before training any models, this preprocessing is performed:

```
> magic_pp <- preProcess(magic_train, method = c("center",
                                            "scale"))
> magic_train_pp <- predict(magic_pp, magic_train)
> magic_train_df_pp <- cbind(magic_train_pp,
                           CLASS = magic_train_output)
> magic_test_pp <- predict(magic_pp, magic_test)
```

Training

Boosting is designed to work best with weak learners, so a very small number of hidden neurons in the model's hidden layer are used.

Concretely, we will begin with the simplest possible multilayer perceptron that uses a single hidden neuron. To understand the effect of using boosting, a baseline performance is established by training a single neural network (and measuring its performance).

This is to accomplish the following:

```
> library(nnet)
> n_model <- nnet(CLASS ~ ., data = magic_train_df_pp, size = 1)
> n_test_predictions <- predict(n_model, magic_test_pp,
                              type = "class")
> (n_test_accuracy <- mean(n_test_predictions ==
                          magic_test_output))
[1] 0.7948988
```

This establishes that we have a baseline accuracy of around 79.5 percent. Not too bad, but can boost to improve upon this score?

To that end, the function `AdaBoostNN()`, which is shown as follows, is used. This function will take input from a data frame, the name of the output variable, the number of single hidden layer neural network models to be built, and finally, the number of hidden units these neural networks will have.

The function will then implement the AdaBoost algorithm and return a list of models with their corresponding weights.

Here is the function:

```
AdaBoostNN <- function(training_data, output_column, M,
                      hidden_units) {
  require("nnet")
  models <- list()
  alphas <- list()
  n <- nrow(training_data)
```

```
model_formula <- as.formula(paste(output_column, '~ .', sep = ''))
w <- rep((1/n), n)
for (m in 1:M) {
    model <- nnet(model_formula, data = training_data,
                  size = hidden_units, weights = w)
    models[[m]] <- model
    predictions <- as.numeric(predict(model,
                    training_data[, -which(names(training_data) ==
                    output_column)], type = "class"))
    errors <- predictions != training_data[, output_column]
    error_rate <- sum(w * as.numeric(errors)) / sum(w)
    alpha <- 0.5 * log((1 - error_rate) / error_rate)
    alphas[[m]] <- alpha
    temp_w <- mapply(function(x, y) if (y) { x * exp(alpha) }
                     else { x * exp(-alpha)}, w, errors)
    w <- temp_w / sum(temp_w)
}
return(list(models = models, alphas = unlist(alphas)))
}
```

The preceding function uses the following logic:

1. First, initialize empty lists of models and model weights (`alphas`). Compute the number of observations in the training data, storing this in the variable n. The name of the output column provided is then used to create a formula that describes the neural network that will be built.

2. In the dataset used, this formula will be CLASS ~ ., meaning that the neural network will compute CLASS as a function of all the other columns as input features.

3. Next, initialize the weights vector and define a loop that will run for M iterations in order to build M models.

4. In every iteration, the first step is to use the current setting of the weights vector to train a neural network using as many hidden units as specified in the input, `hidden_units`.

5. Then, compute a vector of predictions that the model generates on the training data using the `predict()` function. By comparing these predictions to the output column of the training data, calculate the errors that the current model makes on the training data. This then allows the computation of the error rate.

6. This error rate is set as the weight of the current model and, finally, the observation weights to be used in the next iteration of the loop are updated according to whether each observation was correctly classified.

7. The weight vector is then normalized and we are ready to begin the next iteration!

8. After completing M iterations, output a list of models and their corresponding model weights.

Ready for boosting

There is now a function able to train our ensemble classifier using AdaBoost, but we also need a function to make the actual predictions. This function will take in the output list produced by our training function, AdaBoostNN(), along with a test dataset.

This function is AdaBoostNN.predict() and it is shown as follows:

```
AdaBoostNN.predict <- function(ada_model, test_data) {
    models <- ada_model$models
    alphas <- ada_model$alphas
    prediction_matrix <- sapply(models, function (x)
            as.numeric(predict(x, test_data, type = "class")))
    weighted_predictions <- t(apply(prediction_matrix, 1,
            function(x) mapply(function(y, z) y * z, x, alphas)))
    final_predictions <- apply(weighted_predictions, 1,
            function(x) sign(sum(x)))
    return(final_predictions)
}
```

This function first extracts the models and the model weights (from the list produced by the previous function). A matrix of predictions is created, where each column corresponds to the vector of predictions made by a particular model. Thus, there will be as many columns in this matrix as the models that we used for boosting.

We then multiply the predictions produced by each model with their corresponding model weight. For example, every prediction from the first model is in the first column of the prediction matrix and will have its value multiplied by the first model weight a_1.

Lastly, the matrix of weighted observations is reduced into a single vector of observations by summing the weighted predictions for each observation and taking the sign of the result. This vector of predictions is then returned by the function.

As an experiment, we will train ten neural network models with a single hidden unit and see if boosting improves accuracy:

```
> ada_model <- AdaBoostNN(magic_train_df_pp, 'CLASS', 10, 1)
> predictions <- AdaBoostNN.predict(ada_model, magic_test_pp,
                              'CLASS')
> mean(predictions == magic_test_output)
  [1] 0.804365
```

In this example, boosting ten models shows a marginal improvement in accuracy, but perhaps training more models might make more of a difference.

> As we have stated several times in this chapter, even a marginal improvement in performance qualifies as converting a weak learner into a strong one!

Example results

From the preceding example, you may conclude that, for the neural networks with one hidden unit, as the number of boosting models increases, we see an improvement in accuracy, but after 100 models, this tapers off and is actually slightly less for 200 models. The improvement over the baseline of a single model is substantial for these networks. When we increase the complexity of our learner by having a hidden layer with three hidden neurons, we get a much smaller improvement in performance. At 200 models, both ensembles perform at a similar level, indicating that, at this point, our accuracy is being limited by the type of model trained.

Summary

In this chapter, we discovered statistical boosting, first providing an explanation of the key concepts used in statistics relevant to the topic of boosting, thus helping to define boosting itself.

We also contemplated the notion of using statistical boosting to better understand data in just about every database.

In the next chapter, will again strive to use developer terminologies, this time in an effort to define a support vector machine, identify various applications for its use, and walk through an example of using a simple SVM to classify the data in a database.

11

Database Classification using Support Vector Machines

In this chapter, we will explore **Support Vector Machines (SVMs)**, identify various applications for their use, and walk through an example of using a simple SVM to classify data in a database.

In this chapter, we will again organize the topics into the following chief areas:

- Database classification
- Definition and purpose of SVMs
- Common SVM applications
- Using R and an SVM to classify data in a database

Let's start this chapter with some dialogue around the idea of general or generic data classification.

Database classification

As we've said throughout this book, if the reader is a data or database developer, or has a similar background, the reader will most likely have heard of and be familiar with and comprehend the process of data modeling. This can be (at a high level, perhaps) described as the effort of analyzing and understanding the makeup and details of some data. Then, this data is organized or classified with the objective being that it can be easily understood and consumed by a community of users, either named (those already identified, such as financial analysts in an organization) or anonymous (such as internet consumers). The following image shows the data classification as per requirements:

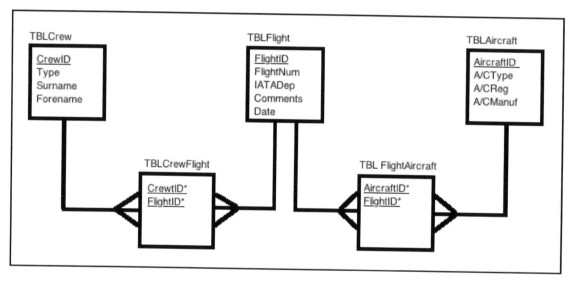

 Anonymous access is the most common system access control method, at least, when it comes to websites.

As part of almost any data modeling development project, one might be asked to create a class diagram. This (class) diagram details how to split data (or a database) into discrete objects, how those objects relate to each other, and any known interfaces or connections that they may have. Each class in a class diagram can hold both data and its purpose.

So, data classification is the process of sorting and categorizing data into various types, forms, or any other distinct classes.

Data classification enables the separation and cataloguing of data according to established requirements for the data, for numerous business or other objectives, so that a data plan or data model can be developed:

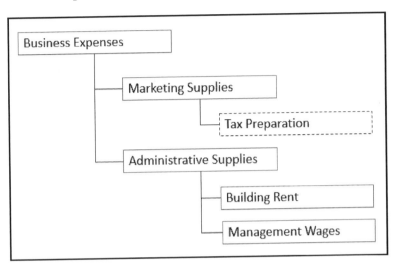

Perhaps a real-world illustration, one which a database or data developer would recognize or be somewhat familiar with, might be the exercise of classifying or reclassifying financial accounts for reporting.

For example, you might find that a typical, recurring exercise during a financial reporting project (or perhaps, during a typical accounting period close) is performing a detailed review of each account, as well as consolidation of the accounts being used, to report an organization's financial results or performance.

To the accounting department, the term *classification* (or reclassification) is frequently used to define moving an amount from one **general ledger** (**GL**) account to another. For example, if an expense (for example, tax preparation) was charged to marketing supplies instead of administrative supplies, the correcting entry might be read:

To reclassify from marketing supplies to administrative supplies.

Here, from an accounting department perspective, we are speaking about an actual transaction to deduct an amount from one GL account and add that (same) amount to another. From a data developer perspective, there would be no account transaction made, but rather a programming change or process would be run that perhaps removes a particular account from one parent (or consolidation of a number of accounts) to another. This is usually referred to as updating the chart of accounts reporting hierarchy, or **chart of accounts (COA)** maintenance.

Will we discover that these same concepts still apply in the field of statistics?

In the following sections of this chapter, we'll answer that question.

Data classification in statistics

Statistical data classification is defined by some data scientists or statisticians as:

The division of data into meaningful categories for analysis.

The database developer reading this should identify with that:

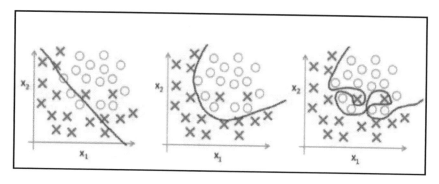

In data science and statistics, classification is defined as identifying to which categories (sometimes called sub-populations) a new observation should be included, on the basis of a training set of data containing observations (or instances) whose category membership has been validated.

 Data scientists routinely apply statistical formulas to data automatically, allowing for processing big data in preparation for statistical analysis.

Typically, a population of unorganized or unclassified data (which is often referred to as raw data) collected in real situations and arranged indiscriminately does not provide a data scientist with any clear understanding, only hunches based upon poorly formed opinions.

The process of data classification attempts to locate similarities within the data and condenses the data by dropping out unnecessary details or noise (which we discussed in Chapter 10, *Boosting your Database*). Classification facilitates the comparison between different sets of data, clearly showing the different points of agreement and disagreement.

Data classification can also help in determining baselines for the use of data.

Classification empowers the data scientist to study the relationship between several characteristics and make further statistical treatment like tabulation and so on.

 A very good example of benefitting from statistical data classification is an annual population census where people in a population are classified according to sex, age, marital status, and so on.

Guidelines for classifying data

The purpose of a guideline (or policy) is to establish a framework for performing a task. There exist many schools of thought on the best way or most effective method for statistical classification.

In statistical data classification, a data scientist will classify data by assigning limits or boundaries. These are most often called **class-limits**. The group between any two class-limits is termed a **class** or **class-interval**.

In your statistical travels, you may have also come across the term *decision boundary*. Data scientists often use different or similar terms for referring to a concept. In statistical-classification problems concerning two classes, they may use the terms **decision boundary** or **decision surface** to define a hypersurface (a hypersurface is a generalization of the concept of the hyperplane) that partitions the underlying vector space into two sets, one for each class. The classifier will classify all the points on one side of the decision boundary as belonging to one class, and all those on the other side as belonging to the other class.

Common guidelines

Guidelines for classification will most often adhere to the following:

- There should not be any doubt about a definition of the classes

- All the classes should preferably have equal width or length

- The class-limits should be selected in such a way that no value of the item in the raw data coincides with the value of the limit

- The number of classes should preferably be between 10 and 20, that is, neither too large nor too small

- The classes should be exhaustive, that is, each value of the raw data should be included in them

- The classes should be mutually exclusive and non-overlapping, that is, each item of the raw data should fit only into one class

- The classification must be suitable for the object of inquiry

- The classification should be flexible and items included in each class must be consistent

- Width of class-interval is determined by first fixing the number of class-intervals and then dividing the total range by that number

Guidelines are applied to whichever guideline(s) or policies a data scientist uses for classification. Those guidelines or policies must apply to all of the data being observed within a statistical project from start to completion.

Definitions

A few key terms that a data scientist must be aware of since they may affect how classification is approached, are:

- **Confidential data** typically represents any data classified as restricted and is often used interchangeably with sensitive data

- A **Data Steward** is usually a senior-level resource whose responsibilities include the overseeing of the life cycle of one or more sets of data to be classified

- A **Hyperplane** subspace; an n-dimensional Euclidean space is a flat, n to a one-dimensional subset of that space that divides the space into two disconnected parts

- **Feature selection** is the act of selecting a subset of relevant features (variables, predictors) for use in the construction of a statistical model

- **Feature space** simply refers to the collections of features that are used to characterize data

- **Statistical classification** is the problem of identifying to which set of categories (sub-populations), a new observation should be a member of

- **Soft margin classification** is a classification where the data scientist allows some error while defining or creating a classifier

- **Institutional data** is defined as all data, maintained or licensed, by a university

- **Margin classifier** is a classifier which is able to provide an accompanying distance from the decision boundary for each example within the data

- **Non-public information** is any information that is classified as private or restricted according to a guideline, policy, or law

- **Sensitive data** typically represents data classified as restricted and is frequently used interchangeably with confidential data

- **Property descriptor**; sometimes a classification system will employ descriptors to convey the reasons for a given classification; for example, middle age or urban are familiar descriptors

- **Interoperability**; when different applications use different descriptors and have different rules about which properties are required and which are optional (for a particular classification), how does that support interoperability?

The reader should spend some time researching the many related terms related to statistical data classification—there are numerous other data defining terms within the field of statistics.

Definition and purpose of an SVM

I support Vector Machines, do you?

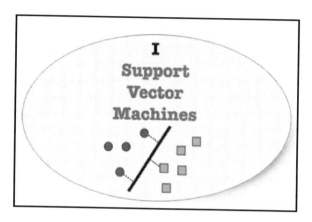

In the field of machine learning, SVMs are similarly recognized as support vector networks and are defined as supervised learning models with accompanying learning algorithms that analyze data used for classification.

An important note about SVMs is that they are all about the ability to successfully perform pattern recognition. In other words, SVMs promote the ability to extend patterns found in data that are:

Not linearly separable by transformations of original data to map into new space.

Again, everything you will find and come to know about SVMs will align with the idea that an SVM is a supervised machine learning algorithm which is most often used for classification or regression problems in statistics.

The trick

You will hear most data scientists today refer to the trick or the SVM Trick; what they are referring to is that support vector machine algorithms use a method referred to as the **kernel trick**.

The kernel trick transforms data and then, based on those transformations it performs, works to discover an optimal boundary (remember, we defined classification boundaries earlier in this chapter) between the possible outputs or data points.

In statistics, kernel methods are a kind of algorithm which is used for pattern analysis. The overall mission of performing pattern analysis is to find and study general types of relationships in data.

Basically, the transformations that an SVM performs are some tremendously complex data transformations (on your data) which then efficiently figure out how to separate the data based on the labels or outputs (sometimes thought of as data scientist defined features) the data scientist has previously defined.

Another key (and thought-provoking) point to be aware of when it comes to support vector machines is that the data scientist doesn't have to worry about preserving the original dimensionality of the data when the SVM performs its transformations.

Consequently, the kernel trick takes the raw data, some previously defined features, performs its transformations, and produces the output you might not recognize--sort of like uncovering a great labyrinth!

The following is from `www.yaksis.com/posts/why-use-svm.html`, *Why use SVM?*:

"You start with this harmless looking vector of data and after putting it through the kernel trick, it's unraveled and compounded itself until it's now a much larger set of data that can't be understood by looking at a spreadsheet.

But here lies the magic, in expanding the dataset there are now more obvious boundaries between your classes and the SVM algorithm is able to compute a much more optimal hyperplane."

Feature space and cheap computations

A huge part of understanding how SVMs work is understanding the trick which we've just mentioned. The trick, as we said, uses kernel methods (which use kernel functions) and are able to perform well in a high-dimensional feature space.

A feature space is an n-dimensional space where your data variables live. Kernel functions are able to operate within this high-dimensional space without having to compute the coordinates of the data within that space, but rather by merely computing the inner products between the images of all pairs of data in the feature space.

This kernel trick can then process the data quicker and more efficiently than if it had to explicitly compute the coordinates. This is known as being **computationally inexpensive**.

For the reader who is a data or database developer, since database views can hide complexity; imagine perhaps comparing the concept of dividing data within a database into several compiled views (rather than running queries on all of the data as a single source) to how vectors are defined and used by SVMs.

Drawing the line

A great way to describe the functional (or the practical) steps that a Support Vector Machine carries out in an effort to classify data might be to imagine that the SVMs are continuously endeavoring to find the line that best separates two classes of data points:

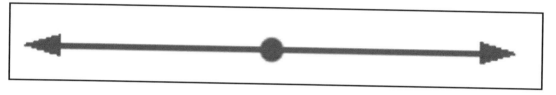

Here, the best line is defined as the line that results in the largest margin between the two classifications. The points that lie on this margin are the support vectors.

The great thing about acknowledging these (support) vectors is that we can then formulate the problem of finding the maximum-margin hyperplane (the line that best separates the two classes) as an optimization problem that only considers the support vectors that the SVM has established.

This means that the SVM processing can ignore the vast majority of the data, making the classification process go much faster.

More importantly, by presenting the problem in terms of the support vectors (the so-called **dual form**), we can apply the kernel trick we defined earlier in this chapter to effectively transform the support vector machine into a non-linear classifier.

 Linear methods can only solve problems that are linearly separable (usually through a hyperplane). Non-linear methods characteristically include applying some type of transformation to your input dataset.

More than classification

Another key point is that SVMs can, in addition to classification, also perform regression.

An SVM using a non-linear kernel algorithm means that the boundary that the algorithm calculates doesn't have to be a straight line; this means that the SVM can capture even more complex relationships between the data points without the data scientist having to do all those difficult transformations by hand.

Downside

So, can we find a disadvantage or downside to using support vector machines?

Yes, sometimes the training time required by the SVM is much lengthier and can be much more computationally intensive (which we touched on with the idea of computational cost earlier in this chapter).

Reference resources

A very understandable book on the topic of SVMs is *An Introduction to Support Vector Machines and Other Kernel-based Learning Methods* by NelloChristiani and John Shawe-Taylor.

Another respectable reference that offers an insightful association between SVMs and a related type of neural network known as a **Radial Basis Function Network** is *Neural Networks and Learning Machines* by Simon Haykin, which we also referenced in *Chapter 5, Neural Networks*.

Predicting credit scores

In the remaining sections of this chapter, we'll try to review an SVMs example based on R thinking like a data developer.

 This example is available online and referenced in detail in *Chapter 6 of the book, Mastering Predictive Analytics with R, Second Edition.*
https://www.packtpub.com/big-data-and-business-intelligence/
mastering-predictive-analytics-r-second-edition

If you're a data developer, you might not be aware that the following website offers a very good resource for test datasets at `http://archive.ics.uci.edu/ml/index.php`

This example uses the particular dataset named *Statlog (German Credit Data) Data Set,* which can be found at the site under `https://archive.ics.uci.edu/ml/datasets/statlog+(german+credit+data)`

The website is shown as follows:

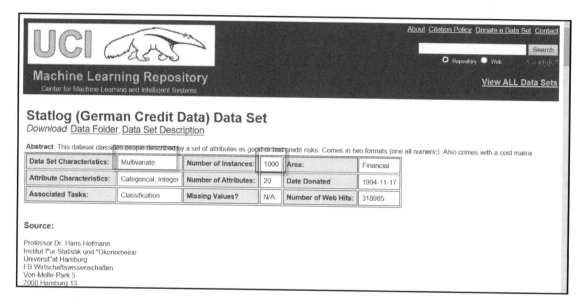

This dataset is data from the field of banking and finance. The observations in the dataset are loan applications made by individuals at a bank.

The objective of this data is to determine whether a load application constitutes a high credit risk.

A data or database developer will most likely observe that rather than downloading a dataset, one would create a query to extract the data as records or transactions, rather than instances (or observations).

 Most likely, if extracting this data from a database, it will not be as easy as merely querying a single table because the loan applications will likely be in the form of a transaction, pulling data points from multiple database tables.

Other points a data developer should consider are:

- Dataset characteristics—field names
- Attribute characteristics—datatypes
- Date donated—the last update or add date

The website `https://archive.ics.uci.edu/ml/machine-learning-databases/statlog/german/` provides two key files; one is the actual data, and one is the data schema:

Index of /ml/machine-learning-databases/statlog/german

Name	Last modified	Size	Description
Parent Directory		-	
Index	03-Dec-1996 04:07	150	
german.data	17-Nov-1994 00:51	78K	
german.data-numeric	17-Nov-1994 00:51	100K	
german.doc	17-Nov-1994 00:51	4.6K	

Apache/2.2.15 (CentOS) Server at archive.ics.uci.edu Port 443

The data schema is in the format of an MS Word document (`german.doc`) and is used to create the following matrix:

Column name	Type	Definition
checking	Categorical	The status of the existing checking account
duration	Numerical	The duration of months
creditHistory	Categorical	The applicant's credit history
purpose	Categorical	The purpose of the loan
credit	Numerical	The credit amount
savings	Categorical	Savings account/bonds
employment	Categorical	Present employment since
installmentRate	Numerical	The instalment rate (as a percentage of disposable income)
personal	Categorical	Personal status and gender

debtors	Categorical	Other debtors/guarantors
presentResidence	Numerical	Present residence since
property	Categorical	The type of property
age	Numerical	The applicant's age in years
otherPlans	Categorical	Other instalment plans
housing	Categorical	The applicant's housing situation
existingBankCredits	Numerical	The number of existing credits at this bank
job	Categorical	The applicant's job situation
dependents	Numerical	The number of dependents
telephone	Categorical	The status of the applicant's telephone
foreign	Categorical	Foreign worker
risk	Binary	Credit risk (1 = good, 2 = bad)

The raw data looks like this:

```
A11 6 A34 A43 1169 A65 A75 4 A93 A101 4 A121 67 A143 A152 2 A173 1 A192 A201 1
A12 48 A32 A43 5951 A61 A73 2 A92 A101 2 A121 22 A143 A152 1 A173 1 A191 A201 2
A14 12 A34 A46 2096 A61 A74 2 A93 A101 3 A121 49 A143 A152 1 A172 2 A191 A201 1
A11 42 A32 A42 7882 A61 A74 2 A93 A103 4 A122 45 A143 A153 1 A173 2 A191 A201 1
A11 24 A33 A40 4870 A61 A73 3 A93 A101 4 A124 53 A143 A153 2 A173 2 A191 A201 2
A14 36 A32 A46 9055 A65 A73 2 A93 A101 4 A124 35 A143 A153 1 A172 2 A192 A201 1
A14 24 A32 A42 2835 A63 A75 3 A93 A101 4 A122 53 A143 A152 1 A173 1 A191 A201 1
A12 36 A32 A41 6948 A61 A73 2 A93 A101 2 A123 35 A143 A151 1 A174 1 A192 A201 1
A14 12 A32 A43 3059 A64 A74 2 A91 A101 4 A121 61 A143 A152 1 A172 1 A191 A201 1
A12 30 A34 A40 5234 A61 A71 4 A94 A101 2 A123 28 A143 A152 2 A174 1 A191 A201 2
A12 12 A32 A40 1295 A61 A72 3 A92 A101 1 A123 25 A143 A151 1 A173 1 A191 A201 2
A11 48 A32 A49 4308 A61 A72 3 A92 A101 4 A122 24 A143 A151 1 A173 1 A191 A201 2
A12 12 A32 A43 1567 A61 A73 1 A92 A101 1 A123 22 A143 A152 1 A173 1 A192 A201 1
A11 24 A34 A40 1199 A61 A75 4 A93 A101 4 A123 60 A143 A152 2 A172 1 A191 A201 2
A11 15 A32 A40 1403 A61 A73 2 A92 A101 4 A123 28 A143 A151 1 A173 1 A191 A201 1
A11 24 A32 A43 1282 A62 A73 4 A92 A101 2 A123 32 A143 A152 1 A172 1 A191 A201 2
A14 24 A34 A43 2424 A65 A75 4 A93 A101 4 A122 53 A143 A152 2 A173 1 A191 A201 1
A11 30 A30 A49 8072 A65 A72 2 A93 A101 3 A123 25 A141 A152 3 A173 1 A191 A201 1
A12 24 A32 A41 12579 A61 A75 4 A92 A101 2 A124 44 A143 A153 1 A174 1 A192 A201 2
A14 24 A32 A43 3430 A63 A75 3 A93 A101 2 A123 31 A143 A152 1 A173 2 A192 A201 1
A14 9 A34 A40 2134 A61 A73 4 A93 A101 4 A123 48 A143 A152 3 A173 1 A191 A201 1
A11 6 A32 A43 2647 A63 A73 2 A93 A101 3 A121 44 A143 A151 1 A173 2 A191 A201 1
A11 10 A34 A40 2241 A61 A72 1 A93 A101 3 A121 48 A143 A151 2 A172 2 A191 A202 1
A12 12 A34 A41 1804 A62 A72 3 A93 A101 4 A122 44 A143 A152 1 A173 1 A191 A201 1
A14 10 A34 A42 2069 A65 A73 2 A94 A101 1 A123 26 A143 A152 2 A173 1 A191 A202 1
A11 6 A32 A42 1374 A61 A73 1 A93 A101 2 A121 36 A141 A152 1 A172 1 A192 A201 1
A14 6 A30 A43 426 A61 A75 4 A94 A101 4 A123 39 A143 A152 1 A172 1 A191 A201 1
```

Using R and an SVM to classify data in a database

Now that we understand the data, we can continue with this particular statistical example.

First, the data scientist will need to load the data into an R data frame object. This example is calling it `german_raw`.

```
# --- load the data
german_raw<- read.table("german.data", quote = "\"")
```

The next step is to provide column names that match our data schema table, shown in the preceding:

```
names(german_raw) <- c("checking", "duration", "creditHistory",
  "purpose", "credit", "savings", "employment", "installmentRate",
  "personal", "debtors", "presentResidence", "property", "age",
  "otherPlans", "housing", "existingBankCredits", "job",
  "dependents", "telephone", "foreign", "risk")
```

Note from the data schema (the table describing the features in the data) that we have a lot of categorical features to deal with. For this reason, a data scientist could employ the R `dummyVars()` function (which can be used to create a full set of dummy variables) to create dummy binary variables for use. In addition, he or she would record the `risk` variable, the output, as a factor with:

- level 0 = good credit
- level 1 = bad credit

```
library(caret)
dummies <- dummyVars(risk ~ ., data = german_raw)
german<- data.frame(predict(dummies, newdata = german_raw),
                risk = factor((german_raw$risk - 1)))
dim(german)
[1] 1000   62
```

As a result of the preceding work, one would have an R data frame object with 61 features (because several of the categorical input features had numerous levels).

Next, the data scientist would partition or split the data into two subsets:

- Training dataset
- Test dataset

This split can be accomplished using the following R statements:

```
set.seed(977)
german_sampling_vector<- createDataPartition(german$risk,
                                 p = 0.80, list = FALSE)
german_train<- german[german_sampling_vector,]
german_test<- german[-german_sampling_vector,]
```

For the data developer, there are similar approaches to take, such as perhaps using the from clause option TABLESAMPLE. With the TAMPLESAMPLE option, you are able to get a sample set of data from a table without having to read through the entire table or having to assign temporary random values to each row of data.

Moving on

One particularity of this dataset that is mentioned on the (previously mentioned) website is that the data comes from a scenario where the two different types of errors defined have different costs associated with them.

Specifically, the cost of misclassifying a high-risk customer as a low-risk customer is five times more expensive for the bank than misclassifying a low-risk customer as a high-risk customer. This is understandable, as in the first case, the bank stands to lose a lot of money from a loan it gives out that cannot be repaid, whereas in the second case, the bank misses out on an opportunity to give out a loan that will yield interest for the bank.

 This is a practical example where predictive analytics have a direct effect on an organization bottom line.

The svm() R function has a class.weights parameter, which is then used to specify the cost of misclassifying (an observation to each class). This is how the data scientist incorporates the asymmetric error cost information into the model.

First, a vector of class weights is created, noting the need to specify names that correspond to the output factor levels.

Then, the data scientist uses the R tune() function to train various SVM models with a radial kernel:

```
class_weights<- c(1, 5)
names(class_weights) <- c("0", "1")
class_weights
0 1
```

```
1 5

set.seed(2423)
german_radial_tune<- tune(svm,risk ~ ., data = german_train,
   kernel = "radial", ranges = list(cost = c(0.01, 0.1, 1, 10, 100),
   gamma = c(0.01, 0.05, 0.1, 0.5, 1)), class.weights = class_weights)
german_radial_tune$best.parameters
     cost gamma
9    10   0.05

german_radial_tune$best.performance
[1] 0.26
```

The suggested best model here has the cost as 10 and gamma as 0.05 and achieves a 74 percent training accuracy.

Next, we see how the model performs on the test dataset:

```
german_model<- german_radial_tune$best.model
test_predictions<- predict(german_model, german_test[,1:61])
 mean(test_predictions == german_test[,62])
[1] 0.735

table(predicted = test_predictions, actual = german_test[,62])
         actual
predicted   0   1
        0 134  47
        1   6  13
```

The performance on the test set is 73.5 percent and very close to what was seen in the training of the model. As expected, the model tends to make many more errors that misclassify a low-risk customer as a high-risk customer.

Unsurprisingly, this takes a toll on the overall classification accuracy, which just computes the ratio of correctly classified observations to the overall number of observations. In fact, were we to remove this cost imbalance, we would actually select a different set of parameters for our model and our performance, from the perspective of the unbiased classification accuracy, which would be better:

```
set.seed(2423)
german_radial_tune_unbiased<- tune(svm,risk ~ .,
   data = german_train, kernel = "radial", ranges = list(
 cost = c(0.01, 0.1, 1, 10, 100), gamma = c(0.01, 0.05, 0.1, 0.5, 1)))
german_radial_tune_unbiased$best.parameters
     cost gamma
3     1   0.01
german_radial_tune_unbiased$best.performance
```

```
[1]  0.23875
```

Of course, this last model will tend to make a greater number of costly misclassifications of high-risk customers as low-risk customers, which we know is very undesirable. We'll conclude this section with two final thoughts. Firstly, we have used relatively small ranges for the gamma and cost parameters.

Originally, when this example was presented, it was left as "an exercise for the reader" to rerun the analysis with a greater spread of values for these two in order to see whether we can get even better performance, which would most likely result in longer training times.

Secondly, that particular dataset is quite challenging in that its baseline accuracy is actually 70 percent. This is because 70 percent of the customers in the data are low-risk customers (the two output classes are not balanced).

Whew!

Summary

In this chapter, we defined the idea of database and data classification using some examples that a data developer may find familiar. Next, we introduced statistical data classification and compared that concept with the former.

Classification guidelines were offered along with several important, relevant terms.

Finally, we spoke of support vector machines, how they work, and the advantages they offer the data scientist.

In the next chapter, we aim to provide an explanation of the types of machine learning and illustrate to the developer how to use machine learning processes to understand database mappings and identify patterns within the data.

12
Database Structures and Machine Learning

In this final chapter, we will focus on the concepts and types of machine learning.

In keeping with the overall theme of this book, we'll start by offering an explanation of statistical machine learning and related concepts, and then move on to drawing out some similarities between statistical machine learning and basic notions that a reader who has a data or database developer background should be able to relate to.

This chapter is organized into the following areas:

- Is a data structure a data model?
- An overview of machine learning concepts
- The types of machine learning
- Data developers and machine learning
- Using R to apply machine learning techniques to a database

Data structures and data models

When you have ample of data, but no idea where It's very important to structure the data, analyze it, and put to good use (wherever needed). In this section, we will be zooming the spotlight on data structures and data models, and also understanding the difference between both.

Data structures

Data developers will agree that whenever one is working with large amounts of data, the organization of that data is imperative. If that data is not organized effectively, it will be very difficult to perform any task on that data, or at least be able to perform the task in an efficient manner. If the data is organized effectively, then practically any operation can be performed easily on that data.

A data or database developer will then organize the data into what is known as **data structures**. Following image is a simple binary tree, where the data is organized efficiently by structuring it:

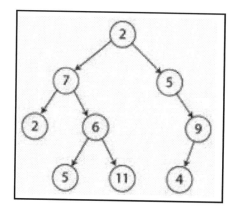

A data structure can be defined as a method of organizing large amounts of data more efficiently so that any operation on that data becomes easy.

Data structures are created in such a way as to implement one or more particular **abstract data type (ADT)**, which in turn will stipulate what operations can be performed on the data structure, as well as the computational complexity of those operations.

 In the field of statistics, an ADT is a model for data types where a data type is defined by its behavior from the **point of view (POV)** of users of that data, explicitly showing the possible values, the possible operations on data of this type, and the behavior of all of these operations.

Database design is then the process of using the defined data structures to produce a detailed data model, which will become the database. This data model must contain all of the required logical and physical design selections, as well as the physical storage parameters needed to produce a design in a **Data Definition Language (DDL)**, which can then be used to create an actual database.

There are varying degrees of the data model, for example, a fully attributed data model would also contain detailed attributes for each entity in the model.

So, is a data structure a data model?

No, a data structure is used to create a data model. Is this data model the same as data models used in statistics? Let's see in the further section.

Data models

You will find that statistical data models are at the heart of statistical analytics.

In the simplest terms, a statistical data model is defined as the following:

A representation of a state, process, or system that we want to understand and reason about

In the scope of the previous definition, the data or database developer might agree that in theory or in concept, one could use the same terms to define a financial reporting database, as it is designed to contain business transactions and is arranged in data structures that allow business analysts to efficiently review the data, so that they can understand or reason about particular interests they may have concerning the business.

Data scientists develop statistical data models so that they can draw inferences from them and, more importantly, make predictions about a topic of concern. Data developers develop databases so that they can similarly draw inferences from them and, more importantly, make predictions about a topic of concern (although perhaps in some organizations, databases are more focused on past and current events (transactions) than forward-thinking ones (predictions)).

Statistical data models come in a multitude of different formats and flavours (as do databases). These models can be equations linking quantities that we can observe or measure; they can also be simply sets of rules.

Databases can be designed or formatted to simplify the entering of online transactions—say, in an order entry system—or for financial reporting when the accounting department must generate a balance sheet, income statement, or profit and loss statement for shareholders.

I found this example of a simple statistical data model: *Newton's Second Law of Motion*, which states that the net sum of force acting on an object causes the object to accelerate in the direction of the force applied, and at a rate proportional to the resulting magnitude of the force and inversely proportional to the object's mass.

What's the difference?

Where or how does the reader find the difference between a data structure or database and a statistical model? At a high level, as we speculated in previous sections, one can conclude that a data structure/database is practically the same thing as a statistical data model, as shown in the following image:

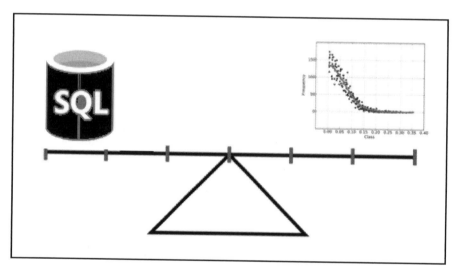

At a high level, as we speculated in previous sections, one can conclude that a data structure/database is practically the same thing as a statistical data model.

When we take the time to drill deeper into the topic, you should consider the following key points:

- Although both the data structure/database and the statistical model could be said to represent a set of assumptions, the statistical model typically will be found to be much more keenly focused on a particular set of assumptions concerning the generation of some sample data, and similar data from a larger population, while the data structure/database more often than not will be more broadly based

- A statistical model is often in a rather idealized form, while the data structure/database may be less perfect in the pursuit of a specific assumption
- Both a data structure/database and a statistical model are built around relationships between variables
- The data structure/database relationship may focus on answering certain questions, such as:
  - What are the total orders for specific customers?
  - What are the total orders for a specific customer who has purchased from a certain salesperson?
  - Which customer has placed the most orders?
- Statistical model relationships are usually very simple, and focused on proving certain questions:
  - Females are shorter than males by a fixed amount
  - Body mass is proportional to height
- The probability that any given person will partake in a certain sport is a function of age, sex, and socioeconomic status
- Data structures/databases are all about the act of summarizing data based on relationships between variables

Relationships

The relationships between variables in a statistical model may be found to be much more complicated than simply straightforward to recognize and understand. An illustration of this is awareness of effect statistics. An effect statistic is one that shows or displays a difference in value to one that is associated with a difference related to one or more other variables.

Can you image the SQL query statements you'd use to establish a relationship between two database variables based upon one or more effect statistic?

On this point, you may find that a data structure/database usually aims to characterize relationships between variables, while with statistical models, the data scientist looks to fit the model to prove a point or make a statement about the population in the model. That is, a data scientist endeavors to make a statement about the accuracy of an estimate of the effect statistic(s) describing the model!

One more note of interest is that both a data structure/database and a statistical model can be seen as tools or vehicles that aim to generalize a population; a database uses SQL to aggregate or summarize data, and a statistical model summarizes its data using effect statistics.

Okay, hopefully, we have successfully presented the notion that data structures/databases and statistical data models are, in many ways, very similar.

At this point, let us move on to machine learning.

Machine learning

There are many deep definitions of statistical machine learning, but let's start off with the simplest or most basic version:

Machine learning is the process that aims to teach a computer to make realistic predictions (or improve on predictions) based on some flow or source of data.

The reader should take note that the data source explicitly depends upon the problem the data scientist is solving (trying to solve). For example, the subscription entertainment service Netflix would not use patient dental record data as input in an attempt to predict subscriber viewing behaviours!

An explanation that's a little deeper can be provided:

> *Machine learning is a sub-field of computer science that evolved from the study of pattern recognition and computational learning theory in artificial intelligence. In 1959, Arthur Samuel defined machine learning as a "Field of study that gives computers the ability to learn without being explicitly programmed."*
> -https://scratch.mit.edu/studios/3475398/
> activity

In machine learning, the data scientist will spend his or her time exploring, studying, and building processes that they can learn from and make predictions on a source of data.

The way these machine learning processes or algorithms actually work is by building a statistical model using example data source inputs. This is different than typical computer algorithms (that is, traditional computer programming) that work by following strictly static program instructions written by a team of developers.

You will find machine learning employed where designing and programming explicit program instructions are infeasible, for example, applications such as image recognition and computer vision.

Later in this chapter, we will take some time and list more examples of where one will find machine learning at work in today's world.

Overview of machine learning concepts

In the preceding section of this chapter, we have mentioned the concept of traditional programming. With traditional programming, the data and program are run on the computer to produce the desired output. With machine learning, the data and output are run on the computer to create a program. This program can then be used in traditional programming.

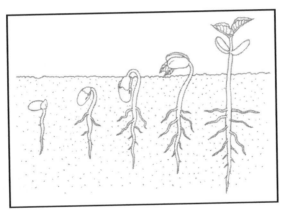

A somewhat popular and perhaps fun analogy for describing machine learning is *farming*.

Here, one might think of the machine learning algorithms used as the *seeds*, the data source as the *fertilizer*, and the data scientists as the *farmers* who plant and feed the seeds and in the end, reap the results!

Key elements of machine learning

There are a good number of machine learning algorithms in use by data scientists today. In fact, some research indicates that there are perhaps tens of thousands. In addition, hundreds of new algorithms are put forward for use every year.

Based on popular opinion, all machine learning algorithms today are made up of three components. They are as follows:

- Representation
- Evaluation
- Optimization

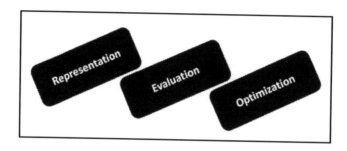

Representation

This is how the information is represented. Examples include decision trees, sets of rules, instances, graphical models, neural networks, support vector machines, model ensembles, and others.

Evaluation

This is how candidate programs (hypotheses) will be evaluated. Examples include accuracy, prediction and recall, squared error, likelihood, posterior probability, cost, margin, entropy Kullback-Leibler (KL-divergence) divergence, and others.

Optimization

This is the way candidate programs are generated, also known as the **search process**, for example, combinatorial optimization, convex optimization, and constrained optimization.

Types of machine learning

Today, there are four types or categories of machine learning.

These types are the following:

- Supervised
- Unsupervised
- Semi-supervised
- Reinforcement

It is important to understand each type of learning.

Supervised learning

This type of learning is also referred to as **inductive learning**. This is where the training data will include the desired outputs; the algorithm infers from labeled or categorized training data. The training data is a set of training examples.

Unsupervised learning

Unlike supervised machine learning, here, the training data does not include desired outputs. This is the machine learning task of inferring a function to describe a hidden structure from unlabeled or uncategorized data. Since the examples given to the learner are unlabeled, there is no error or reward signal to evaluate a potential solution.

Semi-supervised learning

In this type of machine learning, the training data includes a few samples of desired outputs. Semi-supervised learning is actually considered a type of supervised machine learning that makes use of unlabeled or uncategorized data for training, typically a small amount of labeled data with a large amount of unlabeled data.

Reinforcement learning

Rewards from a sequence of actions, **Artificial intelligence (AI)** types like it, as it is the most ambitious type of learning. **Reinforcement learning (RL)** is a type of machine learning that allows machines and software agents to automatically determine the ideal behaviour within a specific context, in order to maximize its performance.

Most popular

Supervised learning is the most mature as it's been around the longest. It is the most studied and the type of learning used by most machine learning algorithms.

Learning with supervision is much easier than learning without supervision.

Before moving on to an illustrative machine learning example, let's review a few machine learning applications.

Applications of machine learning

If it's not clear just yet why the topic of machine learning is so significant, perhaps reviewing a list of real-world machine learning use cases will help.

In this section, we'll take a little of your time to list some real-world machine learning applications.

Sample applications of machine learning that are in use today (in fact, almost every day) include the following:

Searching	You probably use this every day on multiple devices. Machine learning results are used to develop web search ranking pages. Ranking pages are lists of what the individual is most likely to be interested in and click on.
Digit recognition	Given a zip code handwritten on an envelope, identify the digit for each handwritten character. A model of this problem would allow a computer program to read and understand handwritten zip codes and sort envelopes by geographical region.
Biology	Rationally designs drugs on the computer based on past experiments.
Banking and finance	Used to determine who to send what credit card offers to. Evaluation of risk on credit offers. How to decide where to invest money.
E-commerce	Predicting customer churn, fraud detection, and bot detection.
Understanding speech	Given an utterance from a user, identify the specific request made by the user. A model of this problem would allow a program to understand and make an attempt to fulfil that request. The iPhone, with Siri, has this capability.

Face detection	Given a digital photo album of many hundreds of digital photographs, identify those photos that include a given person. A model of this decision process would allow a program to organize photos by person. Some cameras and software, such as iPhoto, have this capability.
Space explorations	Space probes and radio astronomy.
Shape detection	Given a user's hand drawing a shape on a touch screen, and a database of known shapes, determine which shape the user was trying to draw. A model of this decision would allow a program to show the platonic version of the shape the user drew to make crisp diagrams.
Robotics	How to handle uncertainty in new environments; autonomous self-driving cars.
Information extraction	The ability to ask questions over databases across the web.
Social networking	Data on relationships and preferences. Machine learning to extract value from data.
Product recommendation	Given a purchase history for a customer and a large inventory of products, identify those products in which that customer will be interested and is likely to purchase. A model of this decision process would allow a program to make recommendations to a customer and motivate product purchases. Amazon has this capability. Also think of Facebook and GooglePlus, which recommend users to connect with you after you sign up.
Debugging	Used in computer science problems, such as debugging. Labor intensive process. Could suggest where the bug could be.

Machine learning in practice

If we continue to compare data/database development and machine learning, focusing on a typical project, we'll see similarities.

At this point, a rather nice piece presented by Jason Brownlee provides a good illustration of this. In Jason's article, he reminds us that a machine learning project includes more than just running algorithms:

> *Machine learning algorithms are only a very small part of using machine learning in practice as a data analyst or data scientist.*

 You can find Jason's article online at `https://machinelearningmastery.com/basic-concepts-in-machine-learning`.

In practice, Jason indicates that the phases followed in a typical statistical project involving machine learning will most likely be iterative and look like the following:

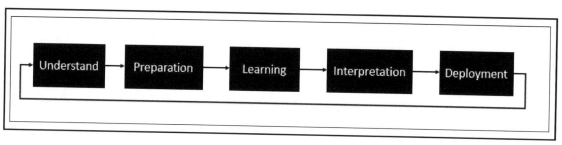

Understanding

The initial phase of the project will involve establishing a good understanding of the required domain knowledge and the goals of the project. The data scientist will talk to domain experts (or subject matter experts) to clarify the project goals. It is not uncommon to have vague or unclear goals at the start of the project. You often have more things to test then you can possibly implement.

 This phase of the project is directly comparable to the first phase of a data/database development project as data developers will always need to gather information from the domain experts to obtain a detailed understanding of the project goals before designing data structures or database models.

Preparation

In this phase, data integration, selection, cleaning, and pre-processing of the data is performed. This is often the most time-consuming part but perhaps the most important step, as it is important to have high-quality data. The more data you have, the more the data is *dirty*.

Again, this phase is relatable to a database development project. System integration, query and selection, cleaning, and other data preprocessing steps (to be able to use it in a new database model) is expected. This will often involve aggregating the data, building key-foreign key relationships, cleansing, and so on.

Learning

This phase is the fun part, where machine learning algorithms are applied to the data.

This phase of the project is most related to the data modeling or data model design phase of a database development project. Keep in mind that in a machine learning statistical project, the learning is more machine oriented, while in a database development project, the modeling is more human-oriented.

Interpretation

In this phase, the results of the prior phases are reviewed and interpreted by the data scientists and the statistical team. Sometimes, it does not matter how the model works as long it delivers good results. In some projects, there are high demands for the results to be easily understandable. Experts will challenge the results.

This phase will relate to the acceptance testing phase of a database development project in that after the database is constructed, domain experts will review and test the model and interpret the results to determine whether the database is providing acceptable results (based upon the requirements of the project established in phase one).

Deployment

In this final phase, the results of the previous phases (the discovered knowledge) are consolidated and deployed.

It is not uncommon for a machine learning project to be successful in the lab but never fully put into practice. More often than not, "another round" of phases of the project are performed, usually with more or updated data.

In this phase, we see the database going live or deployed into a production environment for use by the owners of the data.

Iteration

Finally, Jason also notes that:

It is not a one-shot process, it is a cycle. The data scientist may need to run the loop (possibly redo phases 1 through 5) until a result that can be used in practice is established. Also, the data can change, require a new loop, and so on.

This might be where a database development project varies from a machine learning statistical project. While it is not unheard of for a database project to have more than one iteration of the aforementioned project phases (perhaps to address certain issues identified during acceptance testing), most database projects typically end with a database that is actually used in practice by the owners of the data.

Using R to apply machine learning techniques to a database

We've used the R programming language pretty much throughout this book since it is used by most data scientists and is very easy for people just getting started in statistics to comprehend. In this chapter, we'll again use R, this time to suggest how machine learning techniques might be applicable to a data or database developer.

We'll use a post offered by Will Stanton, a data scientist, to get us started. In his post, he offers a clever example of creating a simple classification model in R, using the caret package.

The R caret package Will uses in his example is very easy to use, containing wrapper functions that allow you to use the exact same functions for training and predicting with dozens of different algorithms. On top of that, it includes sophisticated, built-in methods for evaluating the effectiveness of the predictions you get from the model.

In this example (although it's perhaps a bit morbid), the task at hand is to build a statistical model that has the ability to look at the characteristics of individuals who were on the Titanic, and then predict the likelihood that they would have survived the disaster.

Understanding the data

Data is provided that contains information on who survived and who perished:

	A	B	C	D	E	F	G	H	I	J	K	L
1	PassengerId	Survived	Pclass	Name	Sex	Age	SibSp	Parch	Ticket	Fare	Cabin	Embarked
2	1	0	3	Braund, Mr. Owen Harris	male	22	1	0	A/5 21171	7.25		S
3	2	1	1	Cumings, Mrs. John Bradley (Florence Briggs Thayer)	female	38	1	0	PC 17599	71.2833	C85	C
4	3	1	3	Heikkinen, Miss. Laina	female	26	0	0	STON/O2.	7.925		S
5	4	1	1	Futrelle, Mrs. Jacques Heath (Lily May Peel)	female	35	1	0	113803	53.1	C123	S
6	5	0	3	Allen, Mr. William Henry	male	35	0	0	373450	8.05		S
7	6	0	3	Moran, Mr. James	male		0	0	330877	8.4583		Q
8	7	0	1	McCarthy, Mr. Timothy J	male	54	0	0	17463	51.8625	E46	S
9	8	0	3	Palsson, Master. Gosta Leonard	male	2	3	1	349909	21.075		S
10	9	1	3	Johnson, Mrs. Oscar W (Elisabeth Vilhelmina Berg)	female	27	0	2	347742	11.1333		S
11	10	1	2	Nasser, Mrs. Nicholas (Adele Achem)	female	14	1	0	237736	30.0708		C
12	11	1	3	Sandstrom, Miss. Marguerite Rut	female	4	1	1	PP 9549	16.7	G6	S
13	12	1	1	Bonnell, Miss. Elizabeth	female	58	0	0	113783	26.55	C103	S
14	13	0	3	Saundercock, Mr. William Henry	male	20	0	0	A/5. 2151	8.05		S
15	14	0	3	Andersson, Mr. Anders Johan	male	39	1	5	347082	31.275		S
16	15	0	3	Vestrom, Miss. Hulda Amanda Adolfina	female	14	0	0	350406	7.8542		S
17	16	1	2	Hewlett, Mrs. (Mary D Kingcome)	female	55	0	0	248706	16		S
18	17	0	3	Rice, Master. Eugene	male	2	4	1	382652	29.125		Q
19	18	1	2	Williams, Mr. Charles Eugene	male		0	0	244373	13		S
20	19	0	3	Vander Planke, Mrs. Julius (Emelia Maria Vandemoortele)	female	31	1	0	345763	18		S
21	20	1	3	Masselmani, Mrs. Fatima	female		0	0	2649	7.225		C

This data is in the form of a downloadable text CSV file, which contains several useful variables for each person:

- **Pclass**: Passenger class (1st, 2nd, or 3rd)
- **Sex**
- **Age**
- **SibSp**: Number of siblings/spouses aboard
- **Parch**: Number of parents/children aboard
- **Fare**: How much the passenger paid
- **Embarked**: Where they got on the boat (**C** = Cherbourg; **Q** = Queenstown; **S** = Southampton)

The step-by-step lines of R code required to install and load the R packages, as well as loading the aforementioned datasets, can be found online at `http://will-stanton.com/machine-learning-with-r-an-irresponsibly-fast-tutorial`.

The example given does an outstanding job of outlining both the methodology and the process steps required to create a simple classification model in R, in order to illustrate a form of machine learning.

The methodology used aligns with what we've offered earlier in the *Machine learning in practice* section of this chapter.

The first steps are understanding the problem or challenge, and the preparation, in order to be ready to perform the actual machine learning.

Preparing

In the R example, we understand that the challenge is to predict the likelihood that a passenger would have survived; we then prepare, by loading the data so that it can be reviewed and the appropriate or best variables can be identified (to be used in a learning algorithm):

The post provides the R commands to read on the `train.csv` file, using the `,` delimiter, including the header row as the column names, and assigning it to an R object. It also reads in the `testSet.csv`, and finally uses the R `Head` function to display the first few rows of the datasets where the reader then sees that each row has a `Survived` column, which is a value of 1 if the person survived, or a value of 0 if they didn't (you can see this information in the image of the data file provided previously in this section).

Going on, the example explains that comparing the training set to the test set, shows the big difference between the training set and the test set; this is that the training set is labeled, but the test set is unlabeled. The job at hand is to make predictions on the unlabeled test set and be scored based on the percentage of passengers correctly labeled.

The article also informs the reader that most of the machine learning is really about picking the best features to use in the model. In machine learning, a feature is really just a variable or some sort of combination of variables (such as the sum or product of two variables).

So, in the statistical classification model example, *the Titanic challenge*, picking the most useful variables to use is accomplished using crosstabs and conditional boxplots.

Crosstabs show the interactions between two variables in a very easy-to-read way. In the example, to determine which variables are the best predictors of survival, the R table function is used to look at the crosstabs between survival and each other variable.

Box plots can be handy to identify useful continuous variables. The R example given uses conditional box plots to compare the distribution of each continuous variable in the data, conditioned on whether the passengers survived or not.

In the analysis performed, one can see that Pclass has a strong predictive value for whether someone survived or not based upon the indicated survival rates:

Class of Passenger	Outcome	Survival Rate
Class 1	136 survived and 80 died	63%
Class 2	87 survived and 97 died	47%
Class 3	119 survived and 372 died	24%

Data developer

How does the preceding example compare to a data or database developer? What might be a relatable example?

Starting from the top, suppose you are in charge of a database owned by a gaming company. The company purchases and places various slot-type gaming machines on the floors of their casinos and clubs.

 Slot machines are a type of casino gambling machine with three or more reels, which spin when a button is pushed. The machine is worked by the insertion of a coin.

The database contains many useful variables for each slot-type gaming machine:

- **Theme**: Traditional slot machines featured fruit and bars as symbols, but themes are becoming the predominant feature of slot machine games
- **Denomination**: Five cents, 10 cents, 25 cents, 50 cents, and so on
- **Payout frequency**: Loose, medium, or tight
- **Player position**: Low-level or upright
- **Reel type**: Mechanical or virtual
- **Number of players**: Standalone or community

Here, our challenge is to predict whether a particular machine will be a popular machine for the gaming company or not, based on the machine's characteristics, or known variables.

In the R example, the data scientist was fortunate enough to have a data file provided. As a data or database developer, though, we're usually not that lucky, although this really isn't such a big deal.

Knowing the data structures/database model (as we discussed at the start of this chapter), the data developer can construct appropriate SQL queries to locate the data we might be interested in for our project (some refer to this process as mining the data).

> Data mining is the process of discovering patterns in data involving methods at the intersection of artificial intelligence, machine learning, statistics, and database systems.

Additionally, once the data has been located within the database, it is a routine matter to write the information to a CSV text file to be consumed by our statistical project:

```
select * into outfile 'd:/report.csv' fields terminated by ',' from
tableName;
```

But in fact, the data developer might actually go as far as performing the data analyses, variable review, and feature selection on the data while the data is still in the database; that way, once the strongest predictors are identified, others (considered to be perhaps noise in the context of our challenge) would not have to be extracted into our file. This saves time and makes the data perhaps a bit more manageable.

> *Noise* was covered in `Chapter 10`, *Boosting and Your Database*.

Understanding the challenge

After fully understanding the challenge at hand, perhaps we have come to know that if a gaming machine type has an average coin-in (the total dollar amount of the coins played on a slot machine) value of more than ten thousand dollars per day, it is considered by the organization to be a popular gaming machine.

With this information in mind, we can construct a query (or most likely, several) designed to calculate and pull this variable's amount for each of our machine observations.

At that point, we would have data with observations (records) for each machine in service by the company, along with a list of each machine's characteristics (the variables we want to examine), as well as the determined result (popular or not).

Sound familiar? It should!

Suppose in our database example we see that denomination is the strongest predictor of whether a gaming machine is a popular machine or not:

Denomination	Outcome/average coin-in value	Popular
10 cents	$7,500	No
25 cents	$18,000	Yes
50 cents	$9,000	No

We can see from the comparison of these examples that there are plenty of opportunities for data developers to locate and use information stored within databases as input to statistical models.

Cross-tabbing and plotting

We previously stated that crosstabs were used to show the interactions between two variables in a very easy to read format. To look at the crosstabs between `Survived` and each other variable, the R function table was used.

Data developers have a similar tool, PIVOT. PIVOT is one of the new relational operators introduced in SQL Server 2005. It provides an easy mechanism in SQL Server to transform rows into columns.

The R example we are focusing on here also used *box plot visualizations* to identify continuous variables within the data. Although native SQL doesn't really provide us with plotting abilities, the data developer might consider leveraging something like **SQL Server Reporting Services (SSRS)** to plot the data mined from the database; however, since the next phase will require us to create a classification model, I would suggest leveraging the visualization power of R to create our charts and graphs.

There is an excellent resource online that is worthy of the reader's time, and deals with the topic *Create graphs and plots using SQL and R (walkthrough)*:

```
https://docs.microsoft.com/en-us/sql/advanced-analytics/tutorials/walkthrough-
create-graphs-and-plots-using-r
```

At this point, you can move on to the learning, evaluation, and deployment phases we discussed earlier.

Summary

In this chapter, we started out by reviewing the idea of data structures, data models, and databases, and found similarities and differences between them.

Next, we provided an overview of machine learning and related concepts, and then compared the practice of a machine learning statistical project to a database development project.

Finally, we touched on a conceptual use of R and applying machine learning techniques to data from a database.

As this book was aimed at helping the typical data or database developer transition into the world of statistics, we hope the reader has established a sound understanding of the relevant topics in statistics and data science.

Good luck!

Index

Made in the USA
San Bernardino, CA
09 November 2018